Praise for other books by Michael W Lucas

PAM Mastery

"Michael W Lucas nailed it." —*nixCraft*

"Fantastic." —*Kris Moore, BSDNow #171*

Networking for Systems Administrators

"There is a lot of useful information packed into this book. I recommend it!" — *Sunday Morning Linux Review, episode 145*

After reading this book, you'll have a strong footing in networking. Lucas explains concepts in practical ways; he makes sure to teach tools in both Unix/Linux and Windows; and he gives you the terms you'll use to explain what you're seeing to the network folks. Along the way there's a lot of hard-won knowledge sprinkled throughout…" — *Slashdot*

FreeBSD Mastery: Specialty Filesystems

"a joy and treasure to read" — *Vivek Gite, nixCraft*

"I'm a fan of his books… he presents them in a way that makes them much more understandable. He has the right mix of humor and information." — *Sunday Morning Linux Review*

Sudo Mastery

"It's awesome, it's Lucas, it's sudo. Buy it now." — *Slashdot*

"Michael W Lucas has always been one of my favorite authors because he brings exceptional narrative to information that has the potential to be rather boring. Sudo Mastery is no exception." — *Chris Sanders, author of Practical Packet Analysis*

Absolute OpenBSD, 2nd Edition

"Michael Lucas has done it again." — *cryptednets.org*

"After 13 years of using OpenBSD, I learned something new and useful!" — *Peter Hessler, OpenBSD Journal*

"This is truly an excellent book. It's full of essential material on OpenBSD presented with a sense of humor and an obvious deep knowledge of how this OS works. If you're coming to this book from a Unix background of any kind, you're going to find what you need to quickly become fluent in OpenBSD – both how it works and how to manage it with expertise. I doubt that a better book on OpenBSD could be written." — *Sandra Henry-Stocker, ITWorld.com*

"It quickly becomes clear that Michael actually uses OpenBSD and is not a hired gun with a set word count to satisfy... In short, this is not a drive-by book and you will not find any hand waving." – *Michael Dexter, callfortesting.org*

DNSSEC Mastery

"When Michael descends on a topic and produces a book, you can expect the result to contain loads of useful information, presented along with humor and real-life anecdotes so you will want to explore the topic in depth on your own systems." — *Peter Hansteen, author of The Book of PF*

SSH Mastery

"…one of those technical books that you wouldn't keep on your bookshelf. It's one of the books that will have its bindings bent, and many pages bookmarked sitting near the keyboard." — *Steven K Hicks, SKH:TEC*

"…SSH Mastery is a title that Unix users and system administrators like myself will want to keep within reach…" — *Peter Hansteen, author of The Book of PF*

"This stripping-down of the usual tech-book explanations gives it the immediacy of extended documentation on the Internet. Not the multipage how-to articles used as vehicles for advertising, but an in-depth presentation from someone who used OpenSSH to do a number of things, and paid attention while doing it." — *DragonFlyBSD Digest*

Network Flow Analysis

"Combining a great writing style with lots of technical info, this book provides a learning experience that's both fun and interesting. Not too many technical books can claim that." — *;login: Magazine, October 2010*

"The book is a comparatively quick read and will come in handy when troubleshooting and analyzing network problems." —*Dr. Dobbs*

"Network Flow Analysis is a pick for any library strong in network administration and data management. It's the first to show system administrators how to assess, analyze and debut a network using flow analysis, and comes from one of the best technical writers in the networking and security environments." — *Midwest Book Review*

FreeBSD Mastery: Storage Essentials

"If you're a FreeBSD (or Linux, or Unix) sysadmin, then you need this book; it has a lot of hard-won knowledge, and will save your butt more than you'll be comfortable admitting. If you've read anything else by Lucas, you also know we need him writing more books. Do the right thing and buy this now." — *Slashdot*

"There's plenty of coverage of GEOM, GELI, GDBE, and the other technologies specific to FreeBSD. I for one did not know how GEOM worked, with its consumer/producer model – and I imagine it's complex to dive into when you've got a broken machine next to you. If you are administering FreeBSD systems, especially ones that deal with dedicated storage, you will find this useful." — *DragonFlyBSD Digest*

Absolute FreeBSD, 2nd Edition

"I am happy to say that Michael Lucas is probably the best system administration author I've read. I am amazed that he can communicate top-notch content with a sense of humor, while not offending the reader or sounding stupid. When was the last time you could physically feel yourself getting smarter while reading a book? If you are a beginning to average FreeBSD user, Absolute FreeBSD 2nd Ed (AF2E) will deliver that sensation in spades. Even more advanced users will find plenty to enjoy." — *Richard Bejtlich, CSO, MANDIANT, and TaoSecurity blogger*

"Master practitioner Lucas organizes features and functions to make sense in the development environment, and so provides aid and comfort to new users, novices, and those with significant experience alike." — *SciTech Book News*

"…reads well as the author has a very conversational tone, while giving you more than enough information on the topic at hand. He drops in jokes and honest truths, as if you were talking to him in a bar." — *Technology and Me Blog*

Cisco Routers for the Desperate, 2nd Edition

"If only Cisco Routers for the Desperate had been on my bookshelf a few years ago! It would have definitely saved me many hours of searching for configuration help on my Cisco routers." — *Blogcritics Magazine*

"For me, reading this book was like having one of the guys in my company who lives and breathes Cisco sitting down with me for a day and explaining everything I need to know to handle problems or issues likely to come my way. There may be many additional things I could potentially learn about my Cisco switches, but likely few I'm likely to encounter in my environment." — *IT World*

"This really ought to be the book inside every Cisco Router box for the very slim chance things go goofy and help is needed 'right now.'" — *MacCompanion*

Absolute OpenBSD

"My current favorite is Absolute OpenBSD: Unix for the Practical Paranoid by Michael W. Lucas from No Starch Press. Anyone should be able to read this book, download OpenBSD, and get it running as quickly as possible." — *Infoworld*

"I recommend Absolute OpenBSD to all programmers and administrators working with the OpenBSD operating system (OS), or considering it." — *UnixReview*

PGP & GPG

"...The World's first user-friendly book on email privacy...unless you're a cryptographer, or never use email, you should read this book." — *Len Sassaman, CodeCon Founder*

"An excellent book that shows the end-user in an easy to read and often entertaining style just about everything they need to know to effectively and properly use PGP and OpenPGP." — *Slashdot*

"PGP & GPG is another excellent book by Michael Lucas. I thoroughly enjoyed his other books due to their content and style. PGP & GPG continues in this fine tradition. If you are trying to learn how to use PGP or GPG, or at least want to ensure you are using them properly, read PGP & GPG." — *TaoSecurity*

Tarsnap Mastery

"If you use any nix-type system, and need offsite backups, then you need Tarsnap. If you want to use Tarsnap efficiently, you need Tarsnap Mastery." *–Sunday Morning Linux Review episode 148*

FreeBSD Mastery: ZFS

"Once again, a great FreeBSD book to read." — *Wendy Michele, nixCraft*

"ZFS Mastery covers what everyone using or administering these filesystems needs to know to work with them every day. It's fascinating to see how the system is used, having seen how it is implemented." — *George V. Neville-Neil, co-author of "Design and Implementation of the FreeBSD Operating System"*

Relayd and Httpd Mastery

Michael W Lucas

Tilted
Windmill
Press

Relayd and Httpd Mastery

Michael W Lucas

Brief Contents

Complete Contents

Acknowledgements

Thanks to Reyk Flöter for being the point man on relayd and httpd, and for pointing out my boneheaded goofs in writing this book.

Anthony La Porte, Stephane Guedon, and Henrik Lund Kramshøj provided their illuminating production configurations. Slices of these appear throughout this book.

Thanks to Josh Grosse for his help debugging Wordpress on httpd.

I did an experiment with this book, offering an auction to benefit the OpenBSD Foundation and get your name in this book. Bill Allaire, habitual OpenBSD auction bidder, won it for $1300. Bill the Web Developer in this book is named after him. As I was writing this book, though, Bill's best friend Mark Allard unexpectedly passed. The website mallard.info is in his memory. For those who think I'm going soft; while I make every effort to be respectful to Mr. Allard, Bill still gets treated with the contempt appropriate for someone guilty of being Bill.

Bob Beck was kind enough to send me the script he used to make OpenSSL generate OCSP certificates. He told me that he'd write a stand-alone replacement tool "one day." I spent a good week in mortal agony understanding the Lovecraftian OpenSSL commands needed to work with OCSP. Right after that, Bob wrote ocspcheck(8), as he apparently thinks "one day" means "as soon as Lucas understands this script." I need to curse Bob for putting me through those tortuous days, but you lot should fall to your knees and offer him your boundless gratitude for preserving you from my fate.

And a special thanks to Liz, for supporting my lunatic way of paying the mortgage.

Chapter 0: Introduction

The World Wide Web holds today's Internet together. Those videos of cats riding robotic vacuums require a whole complicated infrastructure behind them. Reducing that complexity helps maximize meme availability.

The members of the OpenBSD project are masters of reducing complexity. Their signature project, the OpenBSD operating system, is a Unix-like operating system that's only as complex as it must be. They provide several widely-used pieces of critical Internet infrastructure software such as the OpenSSH secure shell server and client, the LibreSSL TLS library, and freely-reusable implementations of other core network protocols. And now they've turned their attention to web services with the web server httpd, the load balancer relayd, and network redundancy protocols such as CARP. These applications have been ported to most other operating systems.

This book takes you through the OpenBSD web stack. The stack is also available on FreeBSD and some other platforms that provide the necessary features. We'll learn how to deploy web sites, balance and manipulate traffic across a server farm, and build redundant servers.

The OpenBSD Web Stack

The OpenBSD web application stack has several components: the httpd web server, the relayd load balancer, and CARP.

The httpd Web Server

The OpenBSD web server, httpd, is deliberately designed to provide exactly the most common web site functions. This means that it might not meet your requirements—if you need advanced server features, this server won't work for you. For a typical PHP application, static site, or download server, it's perfectly adequate.

Why is a minimal web server important? While the Internet existed long before the Web, the Web's pointy-clicky interface was a key part in popularizing the Internet. The Web's core protocols have evolved since their introduction in 1991. Some things that looked like great ideas on paper turned out to be complete sewage once exposed to actual users. Other protocol components worked well in the age of 33.6 modems, but are nearly irrelevant today. The code to support those features remains in most web servers, however.

The minimal feature set extends to the configuration. The most sensible features are not optional, but mandatory. For example, the smart way to run a web site is to restrict it to a subsection of the server's filesystem (a chroot). Httpd always runs in a chroot. You cannot turn that feature off. If you want to reduce system security, you must run a less secure web server.

Even if you can't use httpd, other components of the OpenBSD web stack can help you make your site more robust.

The PF packet filter

Once you get beyond httpd into the reliability options, the stack makes heavy use of OpenBSD's packet filter, PF. PF is a general-purpose packet filter that allows you to dictate which traffic a host accepts and rejects based on its TCP/IP characteristics. It performs network address translation (NAT) and can do traffic shaping.

PF includes its own load balancing algorithm. It is completely fault-intolerant, however, so we won't spend any time on it. You're much better off proceeding directly to relayd.

The relayd Load Balancer

If you have a large web site, you'll probably have to split the load between several web servers. Relayd is a tool for redirecting traffic between servers, letting you divide traffic between multiple hosts. While we mostly discuss web site load balancing, you can use relayd to configure load balancing for any TCP/IP protocol.

In addition to distributing load between servers, relayd can act as a web proxy, letting you intercept and filter traffic from desktop clients.

Relayd has features unrelated to the web stack, such as the ability to dynamically load balance multiple Internet links. They're worthy of attention, but less widely useful, so this book won't cover them.

The Common Address Redundancy Protocol

If your site isn't large enough to merit a server farm and load balancer, but you still want redundancy against hardware failures, then the Common Address Redundancy Protocol, or CARP, is your friend. CARP allows multiple hosts to share a single IP address. If one of the hosts fails, the other can take over providing service. This means that as you're replacing one host, your web site stays up. CARP is a great way to provide high availability to a service like the Web.

Why the OpenBSD Stack?

Server software follows a predictable life cycle. Someone writes a handy tool to provide a service. The tool gains a following. People add features to make the tool even more useful, increasing its popularity. Eventually the software grows a thick manual worth of features, and any grace or elegance found in the original tool is long buried under layer upon layer of software barnacles.

That, of course, is when someone else writes a small tool to easily and simply do the original thing. It's the circle of digital life.

OpenBSD has a long-standing practice of standing athwart software development, yelling "Stop!" They stick by the original Unix principles of small tools that each do one thing well. Rather than a wish list of features to be added to relayd and httpd, the primary author maintains a list of features that will never be added to the software, as well as a much shorter list of things that could conceivably be added if the right implementation appears. This gives users a realistic ability to decide if httpd meets their needs, or if they should move on to one of the other servers.

Stack Limitations

This stripped-down approach has limits. While httpd, relayd, and CARP are excellent solutions for many sites, they don't support functions some organizations require. If you need any of these features, you're better off choosing an alternate solution.

The developers have made explicit decisions to not support certain features. Httpd will never support rewrites with Perl-style regular expressions, for example. Perl regexes have grown features for decades, and are now incredibly complicated. The code to support them would vastly increase the size of the httpd code and make it both less maintainable and less secure. Httpd includes Lua pattern support, though, which are simpler but almost as flexible. It *might* develop support for rewrites using Lua patterns, but the rewrite code has not appeared as of this book's release date.

You can't define your own custom log formats for httpd—you're stuck with the formats used by 99% of the web servers and 100% of the log analyzers.

Any of these drawbacks could be eliminated by writing the code for the feature, of course. If you wind up modifying some of the software, be sure to submit your patches to the software authors. Yes, they might turn down the feature. (If you submit code to support Perl regexes, they'll *certainly* reject it.) But having the patches available might help other people.

Web Browsers and Testing

Testing a configuration is a vital part of learning any sysadmin task. The usual way to test web servers is with a web browser. Not all web browsers are equal, however. If you get inexplicable behavior with one browser, try another.

As I was writing the part of this book on httpd virtual servers, I learned that the particular version of Firefox that I'd been auto-updated to that week showed me sites from its cache even when explicitly told not to. With the next set of updates, though, Firefox worked as I expected. Next week, Chrome will start doing something boneheaded.

When your web site seems to behave oddly, try a different browser.

Sadly, the most reliable browsers I've found for testing any web server stack are the text-only ones. I'm partial to Lynx, if only because that was the first browser I ever used, but links and w3m seem just as reliable.

Reference Platforms

We'll mostly work with the web stack's native platform, OpenBSD. These applications have been ported to other platforms, such as FreeBSD, and most of the information herein is applicable there.

The relayd load balancer depends on the PF firewall. PF is not available on Linux, except in hybrids like Debian GNU/kFreeBSD. I expect that someone will port all of these applications to Linux at some point, but I cannot anticipate what compromises they will have to make or the performance of such a port.

Web providers abuse the word "server" even more than the rest of the IT industry does. A piece of hardware might be called a server. An operating system installation might be called a server, particularly in a virtualized environment. The httpd software suite is called a server. And now, a single web site provided by that suite is called a server. Additionally, the term "virtual server" is currently used to mean "operating system installation on virtual hardware" or "single web site running on the web site software suite."

When discussing web services, this book reserves both "server" and "virtual server" for web sites run on httpd. Httpd runs on an operating system instance. I don't care if that's on bare metal or virtualized. When I discuss relayd, though, the word "server" means the operating system instance, because "operating system instance" is long and clunky and can't even be unambiguously acronymed.

FreeBSD and the OpenBSD Web Stack

While this book uses OpenBSD as its reference platform, you can run the entire stack on FreeBSD. Some of the underlying system configuration differs, such as CARP devices, but the fundamentals of how things work discussed herein are applicable.

FreeBSD supports the kernel-level requirements of the OpenBSD web stack, but there's one userland concern: TLS. FreeBSD uses the traditional OpenSSL TLS library. OpenBSD builds everything on top of the more secure LibreSSL TLS library. While LibreSSL deliberately supports much of the OpenSSL programming interface, httpd and relayd are built on top of the simpler LibreSSL interface. You literally cannot build these programs with OpenSSL. FreeBSD's precompiled packages all use OpenSSL.

If you want precompiled packages on FreeBSD, I recommend investigating a FreeBSD-based operating system that has completely switched from OpenSSL to LibreSSL, such as HardenedBSD (https://hardenedbsd.org) or TrueOS (https://www.trueos.org).

To use pure FreeBSD and httpd or relayd, you'll need to build your own packages using the ports system. All add-on software, not just httpd and relayd, must be built with LibreSSL. This pretty much means abandoning prebuilt packages and using ports for everything. Tell the ports system to use LibreSSL with an */etc/make.conf* entry.

```
DEFAULT_VERSIONS+=ssl=libressl
```

If you manage several web servers or load balancers, definitely investigate building your own packages with poudriere.

System Configuration

Whatever platform you run, separate your application data from the operating system.

OpenBSD's default installer creates a 2 GB */var* partition, but if the host is a dedicated web server you'll need more space than that. I'd even recommend that you create a separate */var/www* partition explicitly for web files.

If you intend to run a database-backed web site, also create a partition for the database's files. Don't put that partition under */var/www*, as that would be inside the web site chroot.

Whether or not you're using a single web server or a cluster of servers and load balancers, configure PF to protect all nonessential TCP/IP ports. Follow best practices for your operating system.

Load Balancing Basics

Load balancing is when you split a load between multiple hosts. That sounds simple enough, but before you a load balancer, figure out what it is you want to accomplish. OpenBSD includes three load balancing tools: PF, CARP, and relayd.

The PF packet filter includes a load balancer. It's utterly fault-oblivious, however, so we won't cover it except as a part of relayd.

The Common Address Redundancy Protocol, or CARP, allows multiple machines to support a single IP address. Each machine has their own IP addresses, used for management, but the group of machines has one or more floating addresses. Each floating address is attached to one machine at a time. If that host fails the surviving machines notice, pick up the floating address, and begin offering service. CARP is more commonly called failover as opposed to load balancing, but it's in the same category of problems and solutions.

The relayd load balancer is for more sophisticated load balancing situations. One or more relayd boxes sit between the web servers and the outside world. Relayd maintains a watch on all of the web servers, determining if they are ready to receive requests. When a request arrives from the outside world, the relayd machine forwards the request to a machine that's able to process it. While relayd is most often used for web requests, it can also balance generic TCP services.

Load Balancing Goals

Your goals dictate the type of load balancing you want to use.

Load balancing can provide redundancy, so that if one host fails another host can offer the site. This kind of balancing lets you perform maintenance on one host at a time. Most often, this type of load balancing occurs with pairs of hosts. If you want two hosts that take over for each other in a failure, consider the Common Address Redundancy Protocol or CARP.

Load balancing might also provide scalability. Perhaps your site is so busy that one piece of hardware cannot handle the traffic. In this case, you want to share the load between multiple hosts. If one host can manage 1000 queries a second, adding a second brings your capacity up to 2000 queries a second. When demand approaches 2000 requests a second, you add a third machine. This is a case where OpenBSD's relayd comes in useful.

You might need to achieve both effects, though. Hardware redundancy and load distribution require additional hardware. If your web site services 1500 requests a second, and each host can handle 1000 requests a second, loss of one host will crush the remaining host. You'll need to add hardware to achieve true hardware redundancy.

Think about your goals. Talk about them with your organization. What sort of load balancing do you need? Once you have a decision, I strongly recommend documenting it in the manner your organization most expects. You might even need to take truly desperate measures, like writing and distributing an actual business memo. Keep this document close to hand, for when (not if) things go terribly, horribly wrong.[1]

Load Balancing and DNS

All sorts of load balancing require that DNS entries for a site point at the public IP, not at the IP address of individual servers. This would be the floating address if you're using CARP, or the load balancer's address if you're running relayd.

The OpenBSD web stack does not change DNS entries for you, and does not require any sort of dynamic DNS.

The whole point of load balancing is that traffic to a site name becomes ambiguous. The client reaches a web site even when a piece of hardware fails—that's good. Sysadmins though, must carefully differentiate between the site name and individual hostnames. The naming scheme you use doesn't matter, so long as you can keep it straight.

---

1   Assuming you're not the reason things go terribly, horribly wrong, that is.

Prerequisites

This book is written for sysadmins with some experience running web servers. I assume you're familiar with common Unix commands, installing software, applying security patches, and so on. I won't explain the innards of public key cryptography in the section on TLS, so you need to either look that up on your own or continue blindly trusting that it works.

I assume you understand your operating system. I won't show you how to configure VLANs, add users, or install software. People new to OpenBSD might grab a copy of my *Absolute OpenBSD* (No Starch Press, 2013). FreeBSD sysadmins should consider my new *Absolute FreeBSD* (coming in 2018, with karma), my various *FreeBSD Mastery* titles, or any of the other fine FreeBSD sysadmin books out there.

Configure your operating system securely. Hosts should only allow users to authenticate to SSH via public keys. Use complicated root passwords. Configure doas, sudo, or other privileges escalation software correctly. Install only the software strictly required to do the job.

I also assume that you know how to configure DNS for your domain and that you won't be put off by standard web terminology such as HTML. The unexpected appearance of an HTTP GET shouldn't scare you.

Once you get into load balancing, you need some basic network know-how. If you don't know what the abbreviation NAT stands for, go find out before proceeding. Most IP addresses and netmasks appear in slash notation, like 203.0.113.4/24 or 2001:db8:bad:code:-cafe::f00d/64. If you need additional networking education, permit me to suggest my book *Networking for Systems Administrators* (Tilted Windmill Press, 2015).

Relayd implements load balancing through the PF packet filter. While I cover PF configurations specific to relayd, I don't cover the basics of PF. If you need detailed PF assistance, check out the OpenBSD PF FAQ or Peter Hansteen's excellent *The Book of PF* (No Starch Press, 2015).

About this Book

Chapter 0 is the introduction you've almost finished reading.

Chapter 1, Httpd Essentials, discusses the basics of configuring the OpenBSD web server, including virtual hosts and authentication.

Chapter 2, Httpd Blocks and Redirects, covers using HTTP response codes to manage web traffic. You'll use response codes to customize web traffic flows.

Chapter 3, Globs and Patterns, demystifies using shell globs and Lua patterns in web server configuration. Yes, you can use wildcards in httpd server names.

Chapter 4, Httpd Logging and Debugging, helps you customize how httpd records site visits. The debugging features will tell you why the server's doing what it's doing, instead of what you thought you configured it to do.

Chapter 5, Dynamic Content and Chroots, discusses using OpenBSD's FastCGI features to use PHP, Perl, and other dynamic languages on your server. We'll also talk about how to make software function well inside the restricted chroot environment.

Chapter 6, Transport Layer Security, covers getting users that little green lock symbol they value so highly. OpenBSD's acme-client(1) gives you free and automatically self-renewing SSL certificates.

Chapter 7, Httpd Odds and Ends, is a potpourri of other little bits you can do with httpd.

Chapter 8, Common Address Redundancy Protocol, discusses using the CARP protocol to build two redundant web servers.

Chapter 9, Your Relayd Host, goes through the configuration needed to convert a plain OpenBSD host into a secure load balancing packet filter.

Chapter 10, Relayd Essentials, introduces the core components and use model of the relayd(8) traffic redirector.

Chapter 11, The Host Check Engine and Traffic Modes, takes you through the ways relayd can determine if a host can receive traffic, and the ways relayd chooses which hosts to send traffic to.

Chapter 12, Redirections, discusses TCP/IP-level load balancing. You'll configure automatic failover and backup hosts.

Chapter 13, Relays, covers application-level proxies. Relayd can intercept TCP/IP connections, adjust the application-layer-request, and send it on to the server or client.

Chapter 14, TLS and Acceleration, covers using TLS within relayd. Combined with acme-client(1), you can build a TLS accelerator without paying for SSL certificates.

Chapter 15, Relayd as Outbound Proxy, goes into passing your desktop client traffic through relayd as an outbound proxy. You can perform the same filtering on outbound traffic that you would on inbound into a server farm.

Finally, Chapter 16, High Availability and High Performance, discusses bringing eking every bit of performance and availability out of your hardware.

Let's dive into serving web pages.

Chapter 1: Httpd Essentials

While httpd lacks the myriad knobs and buttons of some other web servers, its settings are perfectly adequate to frustrate you. We'll start with a basic configuration, then add options to showcase httpd's core features.

While the httpd program *(/usr/sbin/httpd)* is the actual software, httpd has a whole bunch of surrounding files. The critical parts are the configuration, */etc/httpd.conf* and the chroot, */var/www*.

Privilege Separation

A web server must perform certain tasks with **root**-level privileges. Only **root** can attach to the common web server ports of 80 and 443. Only **root** can open certain log files. Only **root** can read private key files. Unfortunately, processes run as **root** can inflict a whole bunch of damage on the system. Intruders that compromise a **root** process get root level access to the machine.

OpenBSD uses *privilege separation* to divide tasks that require root from those that don't. When you start httpd, you'll get a single process running as root. This process binds to ports, opens log files, reads private keys, and handles all the other privileged tasks. A second process will lose its privileges for everything but handling logs. You'll also get entirely separate processes that handle client requests. A httpd in standard configuration runs five processes.

```
# ps -ax | grep http
54004 ??  Isp  0:00.13 httpd: logger (httpd)
81473 ??  Isp  0:00.01 /usr/sbin/httpd
58369 ??  Isp  0:00.26 httpd: server (httpd)
93246 ??  Isp  0:00.23 httpd: server (httpd)
34118 ??  Isp  0:00.28 httpd: server (httpd)
```

13

When an unprivileged process needs privileged information, it requests it from the parent. The privileged parent determines if the child gets that information or not. There's no reason for the logger to have private keys, so it can never get that information.

httpd(8)

The httpd daemon software httpd(8) normally runs without any arguments and is started at boot or by rcctl(8). You might need to run it by hand occasionally, however. We'll cover some of these in appropriate sections, but here's a couple options to get you started.

There's nothing like the sick feeling of restarting a public-facing service only to get an error message like `Syntax error in line 831` and the daemon completely refuses to run. Validate the configuration file before trying to restart the server with `httpd -n`. If you're testing an alternate configuration file, specify that file with `-f`.

```
# httpd -nf httpd.conf-test
configuration OK
```

If the web server is doing things you don't expect, you might want to run httpd(8) in debug mode. This means that `httpd` won't detach from the terminal, but instead print details on what it's doing.

```
# httpd -d
startup
```

Add one or more `-v` to increase verbosity. Hit CTRL-C to terminate debug-mode `httpd`.

You can manage httpd through OpenBSD's rcctl(8) mechanism, running commands like `rcctl restart httpd` and `rcctl reload httpd`. A restart clears everything from system memory. Reloading tells the parent process to send the configuration and private keys to the unprivileged process. A reload might be slightly faster, but won't let you change settings like prefork and the chroot directory.

/etc/httpd.conf

The httpd configuration file resembles other OpenBSD daemons, with a keyword and value syntax. Curly braces mark subsections, such as settings for individual virtual hosts. OpenBSD doesn't install a configuration file, but you can find a detailed sample configuration in `/etc/examples/httpd.conf`. The sample won't work out of the box—you must set variables such as the IP address and the server name.

Here's a simple `httpd.conf` for my biggest customer's web site, http://www.mallard.info.

```
server "www.mallard.info" {
    listen on 192.0.2.101 port 80
    root "/mallard.info"
}
```

This config defines a server name, attaches the httpd daemon to an IP address and port, and points the server to a document root directory. If your site contains only static pages, a configuration like this suffices.

You can use a configuration file other than `/etc/httpd.conf`. Give httpd the `-f` argument and the new configuration file. If you're setting a new configuration file in `/etc/rc.conf.local`, give the full path to the file.

The next few chapters of this book explore `httpd.conf` in agonizing detail.

The Httpd Chroot

All web site files, Unix sockets, device nodes, and so on must go in a single directory. Httpd uses chroot(2) to lock itself into that directory. A running server cannot access any files outside that directory. The chroot directory defaults to `/var/www`, the home directory of the **www** user. You'll find several subdirectories in the chroot.

OpenBSD ships with an Automatic Certificate Management Environment client, acme-client(1). It's most commonly used for the Let's Encrypt certificate authority. The acme-client program stores its TLS certificates and working files in `/var/www/acme`.

The `/var/www/bin` directory contains programs needed by the BGP looking glass CGI script included with OpenBSD. Without these programs inside the chroot, the CGI script can't work. Note that OpenBSD ships with these files set to mode 0; you must change the file permissions to use them.

The cache directory is used for temporary files. It's most often empty.

Httpd supports CGI scripts, of course. The default chroot includes the `/var/www/cgi-bin` directory for the sample scripts. If your server only has one site, the default directory is fine. If your server hosts multiple sites, though, you almost certainly want each site to have its own cgi-bin directory.

The `/var/www/conf` directory contains any configuration files used by programs within the chroot. OpenBSD ships with the configuration files used by the BGP looking glass.

The default web site goes in `/var/www/htdocs`. The only files included with httpd are those for the BGP looking glass.

The chroot includes a log directory. The logs don't have to be inside the chroot, as httpd opens the log files before chrooting itself. Apache and nginx default to using `/var/www/logs`, so httpd follows their example. Chapter 4 discusses logging.

Httpd uses FastCGI to run scripts, such as CGIs and PHP pages. OpenBSD's FastCGI implementation, slowcgi(8), accepts requests via Unix sockets. Those sockets go in `/var/www/run`.

It's possible that operating system upgrades might change the contents of `/var/www`. You might want to change the location of your chroot, so that you can precisely control what goes on in your site. You might also have enterprise guidelines that define where you must put web site files. Use the *chroot* option in `httpd.conf` to specify a new base directory for httpd. Here I abandon OpenBSD's default and create a new chroot in `/www`.

```
chroot "/www"
```

Now that you know where to find the parts, let's configure some web sites.

Httpd Configuration

All httpd configuration happens in `/etc/httpd.conf`. You can add additional files, but you must specify those in `httpd.conf`. While httpd(8) has sensible defaults for the modern Internet, you can customize individual sites, logging, and server management.

Httpd will not start or run with an invalid configuration. Any time you change the configuration file, validate the configuration as discussed in "httpd(8)" earlier this chapter before trying to restart the service. You can also update most configuration settings with SIGHUP.

Vital functions include per-server configuration, media types, global settings, and macros.

Macros

One of the easiest ways to break a server configuration is by incompletely updating repeating information. Suppose your web server has two IP addresses. One hundred sites listen on one IP, while another hundred listen on the other. Each site has a configuration entry specifying which IP it's attached to. This configuration works fine, until you need to change an IP address. Miss changing one configuration statement, and you break a site. Failed sites mean unhappy customers. Search and replace helps—but anyone who's ever had to change dozens or hundreds of entries knows how quickly the human brain goes numb. Multiply this problem by all the configuration statements that get repeated, and suddenly you have all sorts of potential human errors.[2] Avoid this entire class of problem with *macros*.

A macro is a way to replace repeated information with a variable. Macros must go at the top of `httpd.conf`, before any other configuration statements. If you need to refer to an IP address many times, replace that IP with a macro.

```
public_ip="192.0.2.101"
```

You can use that macro in a configuration. Use a dollar sign ($) in front of the macro name to indicate that it's a variable. Here I use the previous section's web site configuration with that macro.

```
server "www.mallard.info" {
    listen on $public_ip port 80
    root "/mallard.info"
}
```

With only a single site, the macro saves us... nothing. The moment you add a second site, however, the configuration instantly becomes more manageable. You might also put these macros into an include file and share that macro file across several services, not just httpd.

Macro names can only contain letters, digits, and underscores. You can't use a configuration option as a macro name. You cannot use macros for anything that appears within quote marks.

This book uses macros extensively.

Overriding Macros

You might want to override a macro on the command line for testing. This is poor practice in production, but invaluable in testing and debugging. Use the -D flag to httpd(8), followed by the new macro

---

2   They're called "human errors" because humans are so *good* at them.

definition. Here I run `httpd` in debugging mode, and set the macro public_ip to 127.0.0.1.

```
# httpd -dvv -D public_ip=127.0.0.1
```

The command's output doesn't display the macro change, but programs like netstat(1) show a difference.

Virtual Servers

Httpd supports multiple web sites on one instance of httpd. Your typical web farm serves dozens or hundreds of sites off of each operating system installation. Each site is called a *virtual server*.

The server keyword marks the configuration for a single virtual server in `httpd.conf`. Our example `httpd.conf` shows a single virtual server instance. You can add virtual servers until the traffic load slows your server unacceptably.

Multiple servers can have the same name, provided that they listen on different TCP ports or IP addresses. This is most commonly used to configure unencrypted and TLS access to a site. I can't imagine why you'd want multiple servers with the same name on different IP addresses on one host, but if you ever have that use case httpd supports you.

Global versus Server Options

Of httpd's many options, some apply to the running httpd instance as a whole. Others apply only within a single virtual server. Look again at our complete `httpd.conf`, with the macro.

```
public_ip="192.0.2.101"

server "www.mallard.info" {
    listen on $public_ip port 80
    root "/mallard.info"
}
```

The macro *public_ip* is a global option. Once set, it can be referred to anywhere in `httpd.conf`.

The "server" keyword indicates the start of a virtual server. Any options within the curly braces apply only to that server.

This brief example demonstrates httpd's flexibility. Most web servers consider TCP/IP addresses and ports a global feature. In httpd, it's a per-server option. Yes, there's a macro that defines an IP address, but it doesn't actually configure any networking—it's just a convenient variable. Not only can you configure the IP address and port on a per-server basis, you can adjust TCP features on a per-server basis. We'll discuss those TCP options in Chapter 7.

Httpd has very limited global options: macros, virtual servers, and media types. You can also define the chroot directory, set the number of httpd process to start when the daemon starts, and define the log directory. Everything else is a per-server property. You can even override many global options on a per-server basis.

Include Files

Configuration files that include more than a few virtual servers quickly become cumbersome. It's often convenient to split virtual server configurations into separate configuration files. Use the *include* statement to pull other files into `httpd.conf`. You cannot use wildcards in include statements, although this is expected to appear one day.

```
include "/etc/httpd-site2.conf"
```

Traditionally, the included configuration files are named after the site each configures. You'll have files like `/etc/sites/mallard.info.conf`, `/etc/sites/default.conf`, `/etc/sites/openbsd.org.conf`, and so on. Many automation systems expect exactly this configuration.

As we discuss virtual servers, we'll assume that each site has its own configuration file in `/etc/sites`.

Included files can include other files. Suppose you have settings that need to go in every server statement. Statements like listen or setting a log style are often common across servers. You can set these in a configuration file and decrease the number of settings to tweak in each individual server.

```
server "www.mallard.info" {
    include "/etc/global-httpd.conf"
    ...
```

The global configuration file would look something like this.

```
listen on $public_ip port 80
listen on $public_ip6 port 80
log style combined
```

A global configuration file is convenient, but beware overdoing them. I find one include file for TLS sites and a separate one for non-TLS sites to be the best balance.

Virtual Server Configuration

Most of the interesting httpd configuration happens at the virtual server level. While httpd has dozens of virtual server options, the four most vital control the document directory, networking, site aliases, and location-specific settings.

Document Directory

Having a running server is nice, but having the server offer web sites is better. Use the *root* option to tell httpd where to find the documents that make up the site. The site's root directory is relative to the chroot.

```
server "www.mallard.info" {
    listen on $public_ip port www
    listen on $public_ip6 port 80
    root "/mallard.info"
}
```

The HTML documents, PHP scripts, or whatever that make up the site content should go in the `mallard.info` directory in the httpd chroot, or `/var/www/mallard.info`.

Any virtual server without a document root set uses the htdocs directory, as discussed at the end of this chapter in "The Default Server."

Networking

Connect each virtual server to the network with the *listen* statement. A listen statement must define both a network address and a TCP port. Httpd supports both IPv4 and IPv6 addresses, but they must by specified separately.

The easiest way to configure httpd is to have it listen on all of the host's IP addresses, on the standard HTTP port (80). Use * to indicate all IPv4 addresses, and :: for all IPv6 addresses. The *port* keyword gives the TCP/IP port. The common TCP/IP port for unencrypted web sites is 80.

```
server mallard.info {
    listen on * port 80
    listen on :: port 80
    root "/www1"
}
```

To make a virtual server to listen only on a particular IP, rather than all IP addresses, specify the address.

```
listen on 192.0.2.101 port 80
listen on 2001:db8::101
```

Httpd can also use interface names and groups. When given an interface name or a group name, httpd attaches to the primary IPv4 address of that interface.

```
listen on em0 port 80
```

Ports can be specified as numbers, or as names from `/etc/services`. Mixing port names and numbers increases the odds your fellow sysadmins will track you down and smack you.

You can use any of these in macros.

Aliases

Web sites often have more than one name. For most sites, the leading "www" is optional. While the server option gives the site's official name, any additional names can be given with the *alias* keyword. List each alias on its own line, as shown here.

```
server "www.mallard.info" {
    alias "mallard.info"
    alias "ww.mallard.info"
    alias "wwww.mallard.info"
    listen on $public_ip port www
    listen on $public_ip6 port 80
    root "/www1"
}
```

Any client requesting one of the alias names (mallard.info, ww.mallard.info, or wwww.mallard.info) will see the www.mallard. info web site, provided the necessary DNS entries exist.

Indexes

When a client hits a web site, the server looks for an index document to serve as the front page. The traditional index file is index.html. Some people and applications use other extensions, some for technical reasons and some for preference. Use the *directory index* option to tell the server the name of the site's index file.

```
directory index index.htm
```

Some sites have no index document, however. Perhaps the site manager wants the web server to generate an index for users, or perhaps the files should only be accessible to people who know where those files are. Many web servers auto-create indexes unless you turn them off, but httpd doesn't create indexes unless you turn them on. Use the *directory auto-index* feature to enable automatic index creation.

```
server "site10.mallard.info" {
    listen on $public_ip port 80
    listen on $public_ip6 port 80
    root "/site10"
    directory index index.htm
    directory auto index
}
```

This site generates indexes for the user, and defaults to using an index file of index.htm.

Combining Configurations

Take another look at the configuration in the previous section. We use the `directory` keyword twice. Those two entries can be combined in a single line through the use of curly braces.

```
directory {auto index, index index.htm}
```

Is this more readable and convenient than making two separate entries? Perhaps. It might be more difficult to use with configuration management systems, however. Choose the configuration style what works for you.

Many httpd configuration options can be expressed using curly braces. This book uses both methods, as the whim strikes me.

Locations

We often need to set special rules for parts of a web site. A *location* statement allows you to change options depending on the request path—the stuff after the site name. In a link like http://www.mallard.info/awesome.htm, the location is /awesome.htm.

You can use locations to assemble web sites out of disparate directories in the chroot. The standard `/var/www` has a separate directory for CGI scripts, `/var/www/cgi-bin`, but that directory isn't inside any web site directories. You could use symlinks to attach the `cgi-bin` directory to a web site, or use a location directive in `httpd.conf` to accomplish the same thing. Consider the following server, built entirely out of OpenBSD's provided examples.

```
server "www.mallard.info"{
    listen on $public_ip port 80
    root "/htdocs/bgplg"

    location "/cgi-bin/*" {
        root "/"
    }
}
```

The main web site content is in the directory _/var/www/htdocs/bgplg_. The location statement defines the request path _/cgi-bin/_, indicating that the following configuration applies when someone browses to http://www.mallard.info/cgi-bin/. That directory has its own root statement, redefining the root directory as _/_, or the httpd chroot's root directory. This attaches the directory _/var/www/cgi-bin/_ to the web site, even though the web site's root directory is _/var/www/htdocs/bgplg_.

Directory locations that end in a slash (/) apply to the directory and all its contents. If you're talking about files in the directory but not the directory itself you'll need to use a file name, a glob, or a pattern as discussed in Chapter 3. That's why the configuration of our cgi-bin directory here specifies a trailing wildcard.

You can use location statements to change how your server behaves with per-location rules.

Per-Location Rules

Running web servers would be a bunch easier if people were consistent. One of my web developers, Bill[3], is notorious for saying things

---

3   For those who skipped the acknowledgements; Bill Allaire won a charity auction to get his name in this book. He paid $1300 USD to the OpenBSD Foundation for the privilege of having me kick him in the teeth.

like "I want indexes on in this directory only, and authentication here but not anywhere else—oh, and this directory is all PHP, so enable scripts there but not anywhere else."

With per-location settings you can, say, password-protect a particular directory, or turn off logging on a particular type of file. Here I disable index auto-creation on one directory.

```
server "www.mallard.info" {
…
directory auto index
   location "/files/" {
   directory no auto index
}
```

The first directory statement enables index auto-generation for the whole site. The location statement turns it off for any request that matches */files/*. A user that visits http://www.mallard.info will see an auto-generated index if needed, but a visitor to the location http://www.mallard.info/files/ gets a 403 (Forbidden) error. The server lacks permission to list the contents of that directory.

While these examples use directories as locations, you can also use location statements to identify files. We'll see many examples of that throughout this book.

MIME Types

Web site authors can load just about any type of file onto a web server. Both the server and the client need to know how to handle random file types. The HTTP protocol uses Multipurpose Internet Mail Extensions (MIME) types to identify file types. The server uses these MIME types to sent the client hints about how to process the file. That's how a web browser knows that a HTML file should be rendered but a MP3 file shouldn't.

A MIME type definition contains two parts: a type definition and file extensions.

```
text/html     html htm shtml
```

This example defines the application type `text/html`. It's for HTML code. The second part lists three file extensions. When a client requests a file with a name ending in `.html`, `.htm`, or `.shtml`, httpd transmits the file with a note that says, "This stuff is of MIME type text/html." The browser uses that information to know how to treat the file.[4]

Not all files require MIME definitions. Most modern browsers know that files that end in `.html` are web pages. You can't rely on any random browser knowing that, however. You also can't guess what random file type a web site owner might upload to your server. It's best to explicitly define the most common MIME types so that your server can handle whatever your web designer comes up with.

Httpd has the most essential MIME types built into the source code. If you know that your server will only ever offer basic files like HTML, CSS, plain text, images, and JavaScript, you can skip defining types. If your server is anything beyond the most basic, though, one day you'll see something break and you'll return to define MIME types. Save yourself later trouble: set them up on day 1. Definitions in the configuration file override the built-in types.

Use the *types* statement to set MIME types in `httpd.conf`. If you need more reasons to hate your life, you could configure each MIME type directly within `httpd.conf`.

```
types {
   text/html          html htm shtml
}
```

OpenBSD includes a list of MIME types in `/usr/share/misc/mime.types`. It's far easier to just suck these definitions into your configuration.

---

4   Identifying file types by file name extension was bad in the DOS days. I hoped we would have moved past it now, but noooo…

```
types {
  include "/usr/share/misc/mime.types"
}
```

You can define types either with an included text file or explicitly within *httpd.conf*, but not both. I strongly recommend you use the included file.

If your particular server needs a specially defined MIME type, don't change it in */usr/share/misc/mime.types*. System upgrades overwrite that file. Copy that file to another location, include the copy, and make your changes there.

Authentication

Httpd allows authentication via industry standard *htpasswd* files. Tell httpd to require a password file with the authenticate statement either directly in a server description or in a location statement. You must give a password file within the chroot.

```
location "/files/*" {
  authenticate with "/htpasswords"
}
```

This example authenticates users against the password file */var/www/htpasswords*.

You can use define a security realm, letting you define text that should appear in the browser's password box. Not all browsers will display this message, though.

```
location "/files/*" {
  authenticate "Legit Haxors Only" with "/htpasswords"
}
```

Once you require authentication, nobody can access the site until they enter a correct username and password.

Httpd includes a htpasswd(1) program written by the OpenBSD folks. Where Apache's htpasswd(1) can support several different encryption algorithms, OpenBSD's only supports bcrypt. Similarly, httpd

28

only supports bcrypt passwords. If you're migrating to httpd, investigate the htpasswd format used on your old platform before copying the password files over.

If you're manually maintaining the password file, run `htpasswd` with the username as an argument. Enter the password when prompted, and htpasswd will spit out the password file entry. Here I set a password for the user **mallard.**, the account Bill will use to maintain mallard.info.

```
$ htpasswd mallard
Password:
Retype Password:
mallard:$2b$08$Sq5gmhbbZO8YznR1TwEOCuwPPEcepVbymQQ3DB...
```

To make htpasswd(1) add the entry to the password file for you, give `htpasswd` the name of the password file and the username as arguments, in that order.

```
# htpasswd /var/www/htpasswd mallard
```

You'll get the same password prompt. If the user already exists, `htpasswd` changes their password. If the user does not exist in the password file, they do now.

Removing users from the password file must happen manually.

Default Server & Settings

Httpd uses the default server when nothing else fits. Perhaps the client reached the site by its IP address rather than a web site name. Maybe a server doesn't have a document root directory set.

If you're running a whole bunch of different servers in a single instance of httpd, you probably want a default server that redirects to your company page or to a general information page. You certainly don't want a random customer's site coming up when a script kiddie's vulnerability scanner hits the IP of the server. If the host is primarily dedicated to a single site, you're probably okay directing random traffic to that host.

The first server configured in `httpd.conf` is considered the default server. Any client that gets to the host without offering a complete modern request gets dumped there.

You don't have to configure every setting for every server. Any setting missing for a server falls through to httpd's defaults. The most obvious example is the root directory. If you don't give a server a root directory, it uses `/var/www/htdocs`. Some people put all of their server root directories under `/var/www/htdocs`, so that clients who reach the server can hit any web site on the host.

One notable but non-obvious exception is the listen statement. Every server must have its own listen statement; httpd has no way to set a default IP and port for every server.

You can now set up basic web sites. But httpd can also do a bunch of things that aren't so basic.

Chapter 2: Httpd Blocks and Redirects

Not all client requests should get a web page in response. Sometimes you need to tell a client to look elsewhere, or just to flat-out go away. Configure these with blocks.

Blocking Requests

Use the *block* statement to refuse clients. Clients that request a blocked site receive HTTP error 403 (Forbidden). You might use unilateral blocks while performing maintenance on a site.

```
server "www.mallard.info" {
   block
   ...
```

You can also use blocks on a location within the site.

```
...
location "/files/" {
   block
}
...
```

Requests to this directory get the same 403 error.

If you don't want to return the 403 error, tell httpd to immediately reset the connection with the *block drop* statement. The server immediately terminates any request to that location, and the user sees their browser's equivalent of the "The connection was reset while the page was loading."

```
...
location "/files/" {
   block drop
}
...
```

Networking purists probably want you to know that this is an HTTP protocol reset, not a network layer reset.[5]

You might need to override a broader block statement and permit access to a subdirectory. Use the *pass* statement to override an earlier block.

```
server "www.mallard.info" {
  ...
  block
    location "/files/" {
  pass
  }
}
```

Users who browse to the main site will get an error. Anyone who discovers the hidden files directory gets access, however. Never, never consider such hidden directories a security measure.

Blocks have a place, but are not broadly useful. Blocks become much more useful when you add a redirect.

Redirects

A server often need to tell clients "This thing isn't here, look over there instead." This is common aftermath from web site reorganizations. Httpd uses the *block return* statement with an HTTP redirect code and the new target to issue these redirects. Here's how you'd redirect a client to another web site.

```
server "www.mallard.info" {
  listen on $public_ip port 80
  block return 301 "http://mwl.io"
}
```

When someone hits this site, they receive an HTTP 301 message and the URL http://mwl.io. This tells the browser to go to the next site.

_____

5   Because it's not enough to give words like "server" multiple meanings. No, we really *must* use "reset" at several layers of the protocol stack.

You can also use redirects on locations.

```
...
location "/personal/*" {
   block return 301 "http://mwl.io"
}
...
```

A browser that requests anything in the site's *personal* directory
gets a 301 redirection code and the new target URL.

One common problem with the popular web frameworks is how
many of them use different locations for similar functions. Changing
frameworks, or even migrating from one Wordpress theme to another,
might scramble your links. Here, clients that come looking for the old
RSS feeds get redirected to the new location. This particular example
comes from migrating Blogsum to run under httpd instead of Apache's
mod_rewrite.

```
...
location "/rss.xml" {
   block return 302 "/index.cgi?rss=1"
}
location "/rss2.xml" {
   block return 302 "/index.cgi?rss=2"
}
...
```

Redirects like this make it more likely you'll retain your current
subscribers.

The HTTP protocol supports a few different redirect codes. Additionally, httpd has a bunch of macros that you can use to build per-site
redirects. We'll look at return codes first.

HTTP Redirect Codes

The HTTP protocol sets aside error codes from 300 to 399 for redirection. While the specification defines several codes in this range, the
ones we care about are 301, 302, 307, and 308.

301 is the old "permanent redirect" code. The client is allowed to remember that any future requests for this link should go to the new target. To get this redirect out of a modern browser you'll need to delete the browser cache.

302 is used to indicate a "temporary redirect." The browser should proceed to the redirected site, but shouldn't cache that information. The next time the user requests that site, the browser should check the server again. (Strictly speaking, most browsers incorrectly implemented a 302 code with the behavior intended for 303, but that's what we live with so roll with it.)

We also have two newer codes, 307 and 308. 307 is a temporary redirect, much like a 302. 308 is a permanent, cacheable redirect that resembles a 301. Most browsers don't yet support them, but they will before this book becomes obsolete, so let's touch on why the protocol committee created two new codes that look a lot like the old codes.

HTTP codes 301 and 302 allows the client to change the type of request. The client can, say, switch between HTTP POST and HTTP GET. The 307 and 308 codes were added to specifically disallow this transformation, but the feature is only starting to appear in new browsers.

Stick with 301 and 302 unless your application specifically requires a 307 or 308.

Redirect Macros

Httpd includes macros that let you dynamically create redirections based on the client request. These are more useful than just redirecting an entire site.

The macro $SERVER_NAME is the name of the server in the client's request. If you browse to http://mwl.io, the value of $SERVER_NAME is "mwl.io."

The macro $REQUEST_URI represents the chunk of the client request after the server name.

You can combine these for transparent redirection of non-TLS sites to TLS, as shown here.

```
server "www.mallard.info" {
   listen on $public_ip6 port 80
   block return 301 "https://$SERVER_NAME$REQUEST_URI"
}
```

You'd also need a separate server entry for the TLS version of your site.

Other macros are less commonly useful, but might help with your application.

The macro $DOCUMENT_URI gives the request path after the server name, including the leading slash, but without any query string. If the browser requests http://mwl.io/bad.php?user=1, the value of $DOCUMENT_URI is "/bad.php."

The $QUERY_STRING macro gives the HTTP request's query string, useful for many applications. The query string is everything after the first question mark in the HTTP request. It does not include that first question mark. When a client requests http://mwl.io/bad. php?user=1, the value of $QUERY_STRING is "user=1." You might combine $DOCUMENT_URI and $QUERY_STRING to build redirections after rearranging your site.

The $SERVER_ADDR and $SERVER_PORT macros give the httpd server's IP address and TCP port. Similarly, the $REMOTE_ADDR and $REMOTE_PORT macros give the client's IP address and the TCP connection's source port.

Finally, the %n macro is used with Lua patterns, and is discussed in Chapter 3.

We'll use these macros throughout the book to build redirections.

Chapter 3: Globs and Patterns

You might have an application with hard-coded paths and need to adjust them to fit your application. You might have weird things going on with server names. Or maybe you want all directories that contain the string "secret" to be password-protected. Most web servers let you perform such functions with wildcards from the command shell's globbing rules. Globs are useful, but limited.

More advanced pattern matching usually comes from regular expressions such as those found in Perl, sed(1), and awk(1). There's one major problem with regular expressions, though. They're terrible.

Regular expressions evolved over years, adding features as people needed them. Writing regular expressions isn't a black art only because it doesn't require blood sacrifices. The code that parses regular expressions is convoluted and very difficult to secure.

Rather than supporting regular expressions, httpd supports Lua *patterns*. Patterns are similar to regular expressions, and permit you to do many of the same tasks, but patterns are much simpler. They're not as powerful; you can't do some of the recursive magic regular expressions support—but they do enough to handle what almost everyone needs.

Shell globs are another type of pattern matching. You've used globs on the command line.

Httpd can use globs and patterns within server and location statements.

Globs

Both server and location statements support *globs*. A glob is shell-style pattern matching. Just about every sysadmin has seen them, but many of us don't more than the wildcard (*). You can use globs to have one httpd server respond to multiple names, or names that match certain limited patterns.

The most important features of globs are wildcards and character classes. Globs support two types of wildcards: one for single characters, and another for zero or more characters.

One-Character Wildcards

Use the question mark (?) when you want to match a single character, but you don't care what that character is. Perhaps at one point, you had a whole bunch of web servers: www1, www2, www3, and so on. Today, they've all been consolidated down to a single site, but the Internet is full of old links. You want to direct incoming requests to the existing site. You might choose something like this.

```
server "www?.mallard.info" {
   listen on $public_ip6 port 80
   root "/www1"
}
```

This matches any site with a name starting with www and one extra character. Httpd serves both www1.mallard.info and wwwT.mallard.info from this definition.

The catch is, this server doesn't match plain old three-letter www. A question mark matches exactly one character. You'll need an alias for that and any other hostname you want the server to match. You can use wildcards and other globs in aliases.

```
server "www?.mallard.info" {
   alias "www.mallard.info"
   listen on $public_ip6 port 80
   root "/www1"
}
```

You can also use wildcards in location statements. Maybe you have a series of subdirectories on you site that all start with the string *secret* and another character. Httpd should not display the contents of those directories if someone should happen to find them, but rather return an error. Control index generation with the *auto index* option in a location statement.

```
server "www.mallard.info" {
   listen on $public_ip port www
   root "/www1"
   directory auto index
   location "/secret?/" {
      directory no auto index
   }
}
```

A user who browses to http://www.mallard.info/secret1 or http://www.mallard.info/secretX gets either a 404 error, the index page of that directory, or a 403 Forbidden error, depending on if the directory exists or if it has an index file. A user can browse to http://www.mallard.info/secret99 and get a directory index, however. A question mark wildcard only matches one character. You need a different wildcard to match multiple characters.

Multi-Character Wildcards

To match zero or more arbitrary characters, use the asterisk (*) wildcard. The following server matches any host in mallard.info.

```
server "*.mallard.info" {
    listen on $public_ip6 port 80
    root "/www1"
}
```

39

When someone points their web browser at www.mallard.info, drunkengerbil.mallard.info, or any other host name, this server can answer. Note the period before the domain name, though. That means this server won't answer for http://mallard.info. You'll need an alias, or you can change the wildcard to get rid of the period.

```
server "*mallard.info" {
...
```

This matches plain old http://mallard.info. It also matches http://www.reallyangrymallard.info, though. If other people are likely to point DNS for bogus domains at your site, using the period and the alias is probably wiser.

Perhaps you have a vast network of web sites, and you want this site to accept requests for all of them. Even a little guy like myself has several domains that contain my last name. If I wanted to have one server respond to all of those domain names, I could do something like this.

```
server "*lucas*" {
...
```

This server would also respond to requests for mwlucassucks.org. I'm fine with that, but your organization might not find it so desirable.

You can use asterisks for locations as well. Wildcards are very useful when you want to apply an option to a directory and all its sub-directories. Consider the following snippet.

```
...
location "/files/" {
   directory no auto index
}
...
```

Any request to the the directory /files/ on the site doesn't get an automatically generated index. That seems simple enough, doesn't it? These matches are very specific, however. The directory

/files/subdirectory/ doesn't match */files/*, so httpd falls back on the global defaults. To make httpd apply an option to a location and all of its subdirectories, add an asterisk.

```
…
location "/files/*" {
  directory no auto index
  }
…
```

You can use wildcards to apply rules to all locations with a particular string in their name.

```
…
location "*secret*" {
  directory no auto index
  }
…
```

Httpd refuses to generate an index for any directory that contains the string *secret* in any directory within the site's directory. If I set the site's root directory to */secret*, though, it wouldn't match; the root directory is not inside the site.

Character Groups and Classes

Matching any character is useful, but maybe you want to match a specific character or group of characters. Use square brackets ([]) around the characters you're looking for. Consider this server:

```
server "[ab1][cd2][ef3].mallard.info" {
  …
```

The first character of the site name must be either an A, a B, or a 1; the second, a C, a D, or a 2; and the third, an E, an F, or a 3. Httpd directs queries to ace.mallard.info to this server, as well as bdf.mallard.info, 1de.mallard.info, or similar. It won't match fad.mallard.info, though; the characters are all included, but they're in the wrong order. Similarly, it won't match ace2.mallard.info—the hostname is too long.

While globs are case-sensitive in the shell, httpd treats them as case-insensitive. There's no need to create character groups like [aAbB].

You can also use ranges of characters. Letters and numbers have an order, and you can use that order in groups. A statement like `[a-e]` means "match any single character A through E." You can combine ranges of characters and digits with statements like `[a-e1-5]`.

To match anything that's a digit, use the range `[0-9]`. Use `[a-z]` to match a letter.

To invert the meaning of a group, use put an exclamation point in front of the range. The group `[!a-e]` matches anything that's not A, B, C, D, or E.

Httpd does not support the shell glob's named character classes, like alpha and digit and xdigit. Most of these are irrelevant for web sites, as a URL should never include a blank space, a non-printable character, or a control character[6]. Httpd also doesn't support some of the exclusions and special characters, such as using a backslash for explicitly saying "match the following special character." A URL should never contain an asterisk, after all.

You can use these character groups for matching locations as well. We'd previously set up a secret directory that we didn't want httpd to automatically index. But suppose you have two separate sets of secret directories. The ones that end in a number you want to not automatically index. The ones that end in a letter should get auto-indexed. You'll need a configuration like this.

```
…
location "/secret[a-z]/*" {
    directory auto index
}
```

---

6   I won't say you'll never see a control character in a URL. But if you do, it's probably a bad sign.

```
location "/secret[0-9]/*" {
    directory no auto index
}
…
```

These classes work on a character-by-character basis. You can't match all numbers from 0 to 99 with [0-99]; you'd need a more complicated glob for that. You're better off using patterns for such tasks.

Patterns

If globs suffice for your environment, use them. If not, you'll need to move up to *patterns*. While OpenBSD does not include Lua, it includes support for Lua's pattern syntax. Lua-style patterns let you perform more complicated matching and comparison than globs without having to get into the tangled morass of regular expressions. You can use patterns in server and location statements.

Patterns can look a lot like globs. The string w* is a valid glob. It's also a valid pattern. You'll need to tell httpd that a configuration uses patterns rather than globs with the *match* keyword, as shown here.

```
server match "w+.mallard.info" {
…
    location match "/w+/" {
…
```

Without the *match* keyword, httpd would treat these as globs.

Lua patterns work by combining a series of character classes and wildcards. Character classes are either a single character, a class defined with a leading %, or a set like [a-e]. Wildcards include characters like *, +, -, and ?. The example server match and location match statements above, w+, match a string of one or more Ws. The pattern %d%d%d%d matches a string of four digits, while rss%w* matches any alphanumeric string that starts with the characters "rss."

We'll start with character classes.

Character Classes

A character class is a character, or group of characters, that you want to match. Complicated and broader character classes begin with a percent sign (%). When you see a percent sign in a server or location statement, think patterns. We're paying special attention to the patterns useful for web servers: for complete information on httpd's pattern support, see patterns(7). A character class by itself is a pattern that matches one character of that class.

The simplest character class is a single character, such as *A* or *9*. This represents that exact character.

A period (.) represents any possible character.

%a represents all letters.

%d matches all digits.

%g matches all printable characters except for spaces.

%l matches all lowercase letters, while %u matches all uppercase letters.

Lastly, %w matches all alphanumeric characters

You'll see other character classes, notably %c (control characters), %p (all punctuation), %s (all space characters), and %x (all hexadecimal digits). These are not terribly useful for web servers, however.

Building Classes

Patterns let you define custom sets. Much like globs, these custom sets are surrounded with square brackets ([]). Build sets out of the simpler character classes by listing them next to each other. If you wanted to match all alphanumeric characters and had forgotten about %w, you could build a set that contained all letters and all digits like this.
[%a%d]

More commonly, you need a class that matches a subset of an existing character class. Just like globs, specify them with a range. Here we match all the letters except Q, because I don't like Q.

`[a-pr-z]`

You might also need to match an existing class plus something. Remember, single characters are classes. Here I match all alphanumeric characters, plus the at sign and the underscore.

`[%w@_]`

Create a set that excludes items by putting a caret (^) at the front of the list. If I really want to match everything except the letter Q, I could create a set like this.

`[^q]`

These custom classes let you define any lists of characters you need.

Magic Characters

Lua uses certain characters internally for the pattern definitions. We just saw the caret (^) used to build a custom set that excludes items. Custom sets are defined using square brackets ([]). But what if you want to literally match the caret, square brackets, and other special symbols?

To literally match a magic character, escape it with a percent sign. The character class %^ represents a caret, and the custom set [%[%]] represents either square bracket. Match a percent sign with %%.

Lua considers the characters ^$()%.[]*+-? magic. Escape any of them when trying to match them with a pattern.

Wildcards and Pattern Items

Pattern items are a group of character classes, probably combined with wildcards. Wildcards offer ways to say "a bunch of this character." You'll combine pattern items into full patterns.

The simplest pattern item is a single character class by itself, without a wildcard. The letter X matches the character X. %d matches a single digit. %w matches a single alphanumeric character. You don't need a wildcard with this pattern item, because the absence of this character class means that the pattern doesn't match.

An asterisk (*) means that you'll match zero or more of the previous character. The pattern w* matches zero or more lower-case Ws.

A plus sign (+) matches one or more of the previous character. The server name example at the beginning of the Patterns section uses the pattern w+. If someone types a hostname as w.mwl.io or wwwwwwww.mwl.io, this pattern will match. It won't match a string with no Ws in it, however. You will still need DNS entries for those hostnames, however.

Pattern items * and + always match the longest possible string of characters. This becomes important for substrings, as discussed later this chapter.

The – wildcard matches zero or more instances of the character class, but it always matches the shortest possible string. If a question mark might appear in a string, but it might not, you could create a pattern item for it with %?-. This wildcard doesn't appear often.

Finally, the wildcard ? matches either zero or one appearance of the character class.

Don't confuse pattern wildcards with glob wildcards. The asterisk and question mark appear as wildcards in both, but mean different things.

Lua patterns also support the %bxy and %f pattern items. They're both kind of cool, but they're both also complicated and they're not useful for web sites. See patterns(7) for details.

Patterns and Anchors

Let's assemble some pattern items into patterns and see what they'll match.

Suppose you want to match a string of numbers followed by a

string of letters. You don't care how long the strings are, so long as there's some of each. A pattern like %d+%a+ matches strings as diverse as "1A" and "897123htnsoeu."

To match a string of a more specific length, the pattern must repeat the character class that many times. The pattern %d%d%d%d matches four digits in a row, where %d%d matches two. For web sites that file articles by year, month, and day, that's enough to identify parts of the web site containing dated articles.

```
...
location match "/%d%d%d%d/%d%d/%d/" {
    directory no auto index
...
```

If you had to set up a separate configuration for each year, you wouldn't bother.

When used at the front of a pattern, a caret (^) anchors the pattern to the beginning of the string. (If you were paying attention earlier, you noticed that the ^ also means exclusion. Exclusion only works inside square brackets.) A dollar sign ($) used at the end anchors the pattern to the end of the string. Suppose you want to match a location that starts with a year, month, and day, but you don't care about what's after that.

```
...
location match "^/%d%d%d%d/%d%d/%d/" {
    directory no auto index
...
```

When you're using patterns with a location, remember that a location begins right after the server name. They almost always start with a slash. In the link http://www.mallard.info/excellent.html, the location is /excellent.html.

Patterns become most powerful with remembering substrings, however.

Pattern Substrings

Patterns have memory. You can use them to build redirects out of parts of a string. You'll need these substring matches to handle most complicated web site transformations.

Tell a pattern to remember a series of pattern items by enclosing the items in parenthesis. Consider the following pattern.

```
^/(%d%d%d%d)/(%d%d)/([^/]+)$
```

This pattern is anchored to the beginning of the requested document—that is, the $DOCUMENT_URI variable, or "the stuff after the web server name." You'd expect this to begin with a slash, and it does.

The next pattern item is %d%d%d%d—four digits, in a row. They're enclosed in parenthesis, so the pattern remembers them. There's another slash, and then two digits in parenthesis. The pattern remembers this item as the second match. After another slash, we have another pattern item in parenthesis—any character that's not a slash. The plus sign means that you need at least one character here.

You can refer back to these items by using a percent sign and the number. Want to recall the first chunk, four digits in a row? Use %1. The second chunk, two digits, is %2, while the random characters of the third chunk are %3.

How do you use this? Let's look at a real example.

Blogsum and Httpd

The example pattern from the last section matches locations like */2017/01/book-release*.[7] It's the pretty link pattern used by Jason Dixon's Blogsum blogging platform (https://github.com/obfuscurity/blogsum). Dixon was an OpenBSD committer at one time, and wrote Blogsum with an eye towards secu-

---

7   It also matches locations like /1066/09/London-Burns-Down-Thousands-Lost, but most blogs don't go back that far.

rity. Blogsum is still quite popular among many OpenBSD users. We'll use it as an example.

Blogsum uses two sorts of locations: the pretty ones, and ugly ones like `/index.cgi?view=article&year=2017`. Blogsum produces the pretty links with Apache's mod_rewrite. Httpd does not have rewrite support at this time, which makes using Blogsum problematic. You can use httpd redirects with pattern matching and redirects to migrate a Blogsum site to run atop httpd without losing any old links. You will lose the pretty links, but the redirects make all of the old links work.

The locations of the pretty links have the format `/yyyy/mm/name`. The ugly links have the format `/index.cgi?view=article&year=yyyy&month=mm&uri=name`. We need to use redirects to transform links from the first format to the latter. We already have a pattern that matches the pretty links. The parenthesis tell the pattern to remember the year, month, and name. We need to build a redirect from those remembered chunks, using %1, %2, and %3.

```
location match '^/(%d%d%d%d)/(%d%d)/([^/]+)$' {
    block return 302 \
        "/index.cgi?view=article&year=%1&month=%2&uri=%3"
}
```

Patterns retain their memory only within a single match statement. Blogsum needs a few extra patterns for yearly and monthly views.

```
location match '^/(%d%d%d%d)/(%d%d)/?$' {
    block return 302 \
        "/index.cgi?view=article&year=%1&month=%2"
}
location match '^/(%d%d%d%d)/?$' {
    block return 302 "/index.cgi?view=article&year=%1"
}
```

Blogsum also needs redirections for page counts and tags. Each of these only needs a single remembered part, for the search page and the numbered pages.

```
location match '^/Page/([^/]+)$' {
   block return 302 "/index.cgi?page=%1"
}
location match '^/Tags/([^/]+)$' {
   block return 302 "/index.cgi?search=%1"
}
```

Between globs, patterns, and redirections, you can perform just about any sort of link transformation and matching you need. Let's proceed into logging and debugging.

Chapter 4: Httpd Debugging and Logging

Ongoing web server management is dominated by two questions: "who hit my web site?" and "what's wrong with my web site?" Answering either of these takes logging and debugging.

Httpd Logs

By default, httpd logs everything to two files in the *logs* directory in the chroot. The *access.log* file contains activity across all web sites, in the traditional Apache common format. The *error.log* file lists both server and site errors, also in the Apache format.

Complicated servers with multiple sites probably don't want to have all their logs in one file, though. If you have multiple customers, each customer needs their own log file. You'll also want each customer's logs to be accessible to the customer, but not to other customers.

Httpd also lets you log via syslogd. While syslogd normally runs over UDP, and is thus prone to losses, OpenBSD's syslogd can both use TCP and encrypt traffic in transit. It doesn't guarantee delivery, but it's more reliable and private than traditional syslog logging.

Log Customization

Each server can generate its own access log and error log. You can set the log location and format on a per-server basis.

Httpd supports the two traditional web server log formats. The older format is usually called the *common* format, even though large web farms use it less commonly today. The newer format, with more data, is known as the *combined* format and is more widely used.[8] Httpd uses the common format by default. Use the *log style* option to change that.

```
server mwl.io {
    log style combined
    …
```

Httpd also supports the *connection* log style, based on the log format used by relayd. If you have a system to analyze relayd logs, you might want to use the connection format.

You cannot design custom httpd log formats without modifying the source code.

I encourage you to use the same log format on all of your servers. Putting two or three different styles of log message in a single log file makes parsing that log really, really annoying. Alternately, you can give each server its own log file.

Set the access log location with the *log access* statement, and the error log with *log error*.

```
log access mwlucas_access
log error mwlucas_err
```

When you have many servers, using a subdirectory for every server's logs makes the system more manageable. You can put these logs in subdirectories, but you must enclose the location in quotes.

```
log access "mwl/mwlucas_access"
log error "mwl/mwlucas_err"
```

Rotate httpd logs with newsyslog(8). OpenBSD's `/etc/newsyslog.conf` rotates the default access log every Sunday at midnight, and newsyslog keeps 4 logs. The error log rotates every time

---

8   If you're ever thinking of naming your new technology something like "common" or "next-generation," don't. Just don't. Even if it's wildly successful, one day it will be neither.

it grows to 250 kilobytes, and newsyslog keeps 7 logs. After rotating a log, newsyslog sends the USR1 signal to httpd to tell it to start a new file.

If you create your own log files, add entries for those logs to `newsyslog.conf`, modeled after the existing entries.

Now that you can put your logs where you want them, let's see how to not log things.

Excluding Items From Logs

Sometimes you expect an error. Maybe there's an old link to `bogus.html` that people keep hitting because it's referenced in a mailing list posting from 1998. Perhaps browsers keep asking for `favicon.ico` even though this site doesn't have one and never will. You can tell httpd to not log such requests in the access log, making the log easier to read.

Use a location statement and *no log* to not send certain requests to the access log.

```
location "/bogus.html" {
    no log
}
```

A no log statement only blocks items from the access log. Attempted but failed accesses still show up in the error log. You could choose to not log certain successful requests, but that would be daft.

Log Directory

You might find that you need to move the logs away from `/var/www/logs`. The *logdir* global option lets you change the log directory. You must specify the full path to the new log directory, not just a location under the chroot.

```
logdir "/var/www/log2"
```

This is a global option, so it affects all servers.

Httpd opens its log files before locking itself in the chroot. (Strictly speaking, it uses privilege separation to have the parent process open the logs and hand the file descriptors to the chrooted child responsible for logging.) You can use a log directory outside of the chroot. Web server logs can get very large very quickly, so I recommend putting them on a different partition than the main system logs.

To move the logs entirely off of the host, use syslog.

Sending Logs Via Syslog

Httpd can send access and error logs via the syslog(3) interface. This allows you to store logs outside the chroot, or even forward them to another machine. It's a one-line configuration change.

```
server mwl.io {
  log syslog
  …
```

OpenBSD's syslog daemon supports sending log messages to other hosts over TCP, with TLS for encryption. The combination makes remote logging more reliable and more private than traditional remote logging, but delivery of log messages is still not guaranteed. If the logs of a busy server are important, log to the local machine.

You might not think logs are important, but they're vital when something goes wrong.

Testing and Debugging Httpd

Never underestimate a sysadmin's ability to mess up a server configuration. Even sysadmins with decades of experience forget semicolons and misspell *cat*. You need the ability to test httpd configurations before turning them on.

Of all the times to discover that you've broken the configuration file and httpd will no longer start, perhaps the worst is when restarting a formerly-working httpd. Httpd will not restart with an invalid configuration. Test your httpd setup with -n.

```
# httpd -n
configuration OK
```

Most httpd errors state the file the error appears in and the line number. Missing parenthesis can skew line numbers, so if the error isn't obvious look further.

A valid configuration file doesn't mean that httpd will start; it only means that httpd can parse the configuration. If that valid configuration tells httpd to attach to an IP address that's not on the machine, httpd will die at startup. Like most OpenBSD software, httpd doesn't blithely accept obvious misconfiguration.

Sometimes you'll have an alternate configuration file used for special circumstances. It might be for testing, or perhaps for certain times of day, or whatever weird situation you have. Specify an alternate configuration file with -f. You can combine this with the -n flag, to test a configuration before copying it to its proper location.

```
# httpd -nf httpd.conf-test
configuration OK
```

You can now copy your test configuration into place, confident that an unexpected outage won't make your server start up with a bad configuration.

To test a configuration with only minor changes, you can change macro values on the command line. Here I change the value of the public_ip macro to tell httpd to bind to a different address.

```
# httpd -Dpublic_ip="192.0.2.222"
```

Changing macro values is most useful when trying to debug httpd. While the error log will point out the most obvious problems, you have two additional debugging tools: verbose mode and foreground mode.

Make httpd explain what it's doing with the -v flag. Adding a second -v makes it even more verbose.

I sometimes run httpd in foreground mode to debug truly vexing issues. The -d flag tells httpd to not detach from the terminal, but rather print all its logs to the terminal. Running in debug mode disables syslog logging.

```
# httpd -dvv
```

Foreground mode tells you what httpd is actually doing, as opposed to what you thought you configured it to do. Now let's talk about more complicated web sites.

Chapter 5: Dynamic Content and Chroots

Static web content is fine, but most modern sites do some sort of server-side processing. It might be a CGI script, or it might be a web language like PHP. Httpd can support almost all of these.

Many web servers traditionally handle these requests internally. A user requests dynamic content, and the server runs the program that generates the content. That's why Apache has PHP modules. This integration causes all sorts of problems, as anyone who's used Apache's PHP modules will tell you.

The FastCGI interface was created in the mid-90s to let web servers hand off dynamic content processing to separate, dedicated processes. As the name implies, this improved performance as well as reduced complexity. Similar systems were developed for other dynamic content. Today, most high-performance web sites use some variant of FastCGI.

Httpd skips the internal processing and hands everything, even the simplest dynamic content generation, over to a separate process. If you can find software to generate dynamic content, you can use it with httpd. We'll look at a couple common examples here.

Programs that generate dynamic content often need access to programs outside the httpd chroot. Throughout this chapter we'll discuss expanding and maintaining your chroot.

Common Gateway Interface

One of the earliest ways to generate dynamic content was the *Common Gateway Interface,* or CGI. A web site could collect user input, feed that to a program, and feed the program results back to the user. While languages such as PHP have mostly taken over the dynamic content space, many sites still need CGI.

OpenBSD includes a sample CGI program, the BGP looking glass bgplg(8). It's a binary executable, requiring little environment support beyond itself and a couple programs. It provides web-based ping(8) and traceroute(8) functions as well as BGP features, which means almost anyone can use it. Once you get `bgplg` working, you can be confident you understand the essentials of httpd's CGI support.

Getting CGI working requires a FastCGI server, configuring httpd, and configuring the environment.

FastCGI with SlowCGI

OpenBSD includes a FastCGI server, called slowcgi(8). Slowcgi is not the most feature-filled FastCGI implementation, but the missing features aren't needed for generating web pages[9]. If slowcgi doesn't suffice for your application, OpenBSD has several other FastCGI servers in the packages collection. We'll stick with slowcgi for our examples.

Enable slowcgi(8) in */etc/rc.conf.local.*

`slowcgi_flags=""`

If your CGI script behaves unexpectedly, try using `-d` to run slowcgi(8) in foreground mode, in a terminal. You'll get all of the

---

9   We invented a protocol for generating web pages, and promptly expanded it to handle tasks entirely unrelated to the web. This explains everything you need to know about why computers work the way they do.

slowcgi debugging output. Do this in an environment where you can control access to the web site, however—*not* in production.

Slowcgi opens a socket in */var/www/run/slowcgi.sock*. You can set a different socket with the -s flag, but any one slowcgi process can listen to only one socket at a time.

If you run httpd with a chroot directory other than */var/www*, use slowcgi's -p argument to set a different chroot directory.

If slowcgi (or whatever FastCGI server you're using) is not running, all CGI requests give "500 Internal Server Error."

Now you need to tell httpd to send certain requests to the slowcgi server.

httpd.conf For bgplg(8)

Running the BGP looking glass requires telling httpd which requests it should hand off to a FastCGI server. For bgplg(8) in particular, you also must attach the */var/www/cgi-bin* directory to the server, like so.

```
server "bgp.mallard.info" {
    listen on * port 80
    location "/cgi-bin/*" {
        root "/"
        fastcgi
    }
}
```

The bgplg(8) application is present the default document directory, */var/www/htdocs*, so I don't need to specify a new document directory in this configuration. I do need to tell httpd about the CGI scripts in */var/www/cgi-bin*, so I set that as a location.

First I redefine the root directory for */cgi-bin/* as discussed in Chapter 2. When a browser requests anything under http://bgp.mallard.info/cgi-bin/, the root statement tells httpd to serve the request from the chroot's */cgi-bin/* directory.

By including the *fastcgi* keyword, we tell the system to pass the files it finds to the FastCGI server.

That's it for the httpd part. You must also set up the environment for your chrooted application, though.

Environments and CGIs

The point of a chroot is that programs cannot access files outside the chroot. Any files your CGI needs must be included in the chroot.

Httpd ships with all the programs bgplg(8) needs in */var/www/bin*. The permissions are blank by default, however, as part of OpenBSD's secure-by-default configuration. Nobody may read, write, or execute these files.

The main program used for BGP lookups is bgplg(8). You must assign read and execute permission to */var/www/cgi-bin/bgplg* for the web server to run it.

```
# chmod 555 /var/www/cgi-bin/bgplg
```

The BGP looking glass can call a few other programs, such as ping(8), traceroute(8), and bgpctl(8). If you're using those functions, make those programs readable and executable as well. Ping and traceroute run setuid, so they need that permission as well.

```
# chmod 4555 /var/www/bin/ping*
# chmod 4555 /var/www/bin/traceroute*
```

The */var* partition is mounted nosuid by default. You must turn that off in */etc/fstab* if you want these programs to work. Other CGI programs might not require that, so if you're just testing CGI functions with bgplg(8) you can turn nosuid back on later.

The web server user (normally **www**) should not own any CGI scripts or executables. The web server should only own files that the web server needs to write to. Don't give **www** permissions to write to files in the chroot, unless an application specifically requires that.

Finally, if you're running bgpd(8) and want to use the `bgplg` CGI to view your host's BGP table, add an extra control socket in `/etc/bgpd.conf`.

```
socket "/var/www/run/bgpd.rsock" restricted
```

You should now be able to open `/bgplg/` on your server and see a friendly GUI for performing BGP lookups, traceroutes, and pings. Merely seeing the menu means that httpd is processing CGI requests. Even if you don't use BGP, the ping and traceroute functions should work.

This will get you started, but very few of us need a BGP looking glass. And most CGI scripts require more complex supporting software. Let's talk about supporting those programs now.

Living in a Chroot

A chroot contains only the software needed to perform its task. The constrained environment of a chroot is a reliable security tool. It's not the be-all and end-all of security, but an intruder isn't going to get shell access on your web server when your web server doesn't have access to a shell.

Running a web server in a chroot seems an obvious security precaution, but many other web servers make it difficult. OpenBSD previously included versions of Apache and nginx with extra patches to chroot them.

Realistically, intruders don't usually break into web servers. They break into insecure applications. It doesn't matter how tightly you secure the web server if you use it to host a terribly insecure application. By running the site in a chroot, though, you can make a compromised site worthless to the intruder.

The downside of this, of course, is that when a program needs other software to perform a task, you must install it in the chroot.

61

Many web applications want DNS resolution and the local time. If your app is one of those, create */var/www/etc*. Copy */etc/hosts*, */etc/resolv.conf*, and */etc/localtime* to that directory. Do not use symlinks, as a chrooted process cannot follow a symlink out of its prison.

A CGI that requires other programs is more complicated.

Gathering All the Parts

Most programs use shared libraries to reduce program size and exploit code commonalities. A program must have access to all of its shared libraries to run. Even seemingly simple programs like ping(8) and traceroute(8) use shared libraries.[10] The versions included in the chroot are specifically built as static binaries that contained all of the needed shared libraries in one file.

You could build everything your application needs as a static binary, but that becomes difficult to maintain. Instead, you can include the application's shared libraries in the chroot. Let's use that old CGI standard Perl as an example. Here's a basic Perl CGI script.

```
#!/usr/bin/perl

print "Content-type: text/html\n\n";
print "<h1>Buy more Lucas books!\n";
```

This script generates really appalling HTML, but most browsers can render it adequately with only a minimum of whimpering. Copy this script into */var/www/cgi-bin/ad.pl*, give it execute privileges, and run it outside of the chroot to verify that it works. Setting up your environment won't help at all if your script dies with compilation errors at runtime.

Now let's get a Perl interpreter into the chroot.

---

10   Because even seemingly simple programs are not simple.

Theoretically, you could dump the Perl binary into /var/www/bin, all of the libraries into /var/www/lib, and it should link together and run. That gets confusing and difficult to maintain, however, and there's always a chance that some piece of software will choke on an unexpected path. I encourage you to replicate the system's directory structure within the chroot as needed. Perl is at /usr/bin/perl, so we need /var/www/usr/bin.

```
# mkdir -p /var/www/usr/bin
# cp /usr/bin/perl /var/www/usr/bin/
```

Use ldd(1) to identify additional libraries and files that Perl needs.

```
# ldd /usr/bin/perl
/usr/bin/perl:
  Start   End       Type  Open Ref GrpRef Name
  000... 000...    exe   1    0   0      /usr/bin/perl
  000... 000...    rlib  0    1   0      /usr/lib/libperl.so.17.1
  000... 000...    rlib  0    1   0      /usr/lib/libm.so.10.0
  000... 000...    rlib  0    1   0      /usr/lib/libc.so.89.2
  000... 000...    rtld  0    1   0      /usr/libexec/ld.so
```

We can ignore the leading debugging information. All we care about are the file names at the end. Perl needs four files: /usr/lib/libperl.so.17.1, /usr/lib/libm.so.10.0, /usr/libc.so.89.2, and /usr/libexec/ld.so. Create those directories under /var/www and copy those files into the chroot.

Theoretically, your Perl program should now run in the chroot. Let's put that to the test by running a command in the /var/www chroot.

```
# chroot /var/www/ /cgi-bin/ad.pl
```

If you've done everything correctly, the script should run. If a library is missing, you'll get an error. Once the command line works, you should be able to browse to http://yourserver/cgi-bin/ad.pl and trigger the CGI.

If you're using Perl CGI scripts, definitely investigate tools like Perl-FCGI to improve performance and avoid all this rigamarole.

Updating Your Chroot

System updates change the binaries and shared libraries on your system. How do you manage the chroot with those changes?

Theoretically, yes, your chrooted binary should continue to run even across a couple of upgrades. The old binaries won't get any security fixes or performance improvements applied to the main server, however. I would suggest that your web site is the last place you want insecure software. Eventually, kernel changes will break these old programs and libraries—and that break might be very subtle, causing you no end of heartache.

I strongly encourage you to recreate the */var/www/usr* directory tree after every upgrade. Ideally you'd script this. You might even orchestrate it with Ansible or another configuration management tool. The easier you can make chroot maintenance, the more likely you are to perform chroot maintenance.

Troubleshooting

If you have a complicated chroot, eventually you'll hit a situation where nothing works and you don't know why. Troubleshooting a chroot from the outside can be annoying and difficult. Sometimes it's far easier to lock yourself into the chroot and look around. It's a last-ditch troubleshooting method, but when you're standing in the last ditch you use the tools you have.

The main problem with going into a chroot is that it doesn't have a shell. You can copy any statically linked shell, such as */bin/sh*, into a chroot. Upon finishing debugging, you really need to remove it immediately. I find it safest to run the copy, the chroot, and the removal all in one command.

```
# cp /bin/sh /var/www/tmp && chroot /var/www /tmp/sh \
   && rm /var/www/tmp/sh
```

This command automatically removes the shell from the chroot when I exit the shell.

Working inside a chrooted shell can feel very clumsy. Basic programs like ls(1) are missing, but `echo *` works. Read sh(1) for reminders on shell builtin commands.

Running as an unprivileged user would require copying password files and suchlike. It's *possible*—but ick.

Now that basic CGI scripts work, let's look at something more complicated, like PHP. And when I think PHP, I think WordPress.

Wordpress

Wordpress is perhaps the most popular blogging and web site development platform in the world. Note that I didn't say "secure"—while Wordpress has done the work to improve its security in recent years, its tens of thousands of plugins and themes each have their own unique security history. Running Wordpress on OpenBSD will let you leverage some of OpenBSD's security features to help secure your site, though.

Wordpress uses PHP to generate the front-end content, backed by a MySQL-compatible database. OpenBSD provides MySQL services with MariaDB, a MySQL fork.[11] MariaDB retains the MySQL-based program names to ease migration, but don't let references to MariaDB confuse you. Install the MariaDB server and you have a database. PHP is a little more complicated, though. OpenBSD relies on a Fast-CGI-style PHP interpreter, PHP Fast Process Manager or PHP-FPM. Each version of PHP has its own version of PHP-FPM.

When you read Wordpress documentation, you'll quickly realize that every operating system provides PHP packages in different groups

---

11   MariaDB forked from MySQL almost immediately after Oracle bought MySQL, because Oracle.

and with unique names. Also, Wordpress can change their require-ments at any time. While this section was correct when I wrote it, con-sult the current Wordpress documentation for definitive answers.

Packaged Software Installation

Start by installing the needed OpenBSD packages.

```
# pkg_add mariadb-server php-curl php-mysqli
```

These packages will bring along a whole bunch of dependencies, such as the core PHP package. OpenBSD's packaging system lets you select which version of PHP you want. If you don't have a preference, at least be consistent.

```
Ambiguous: choose package for php-curl
a       0: <None>
        1: php-curl-5.5.37p1
        2: php-curl-5.6.27p0
        3: php-curl-7.0.12p0
```

I choose 3, for PHP 7. I must also select version 7 of any other PHP packages, or I'll wind up with multiple incomplete and incompat-ible PHP installs.

The package install will end with a message like this.

```
…
The following new rcscripts were installed: /etc/rc.d/mysqld
   /etc/rc.d/php70_fpm
See rcctl(8) for details.
Look in /usr/local/share/doc/pkg-readmes for extra documentation.
```

Conveniently enough, we want to start both mysqld(8) and the PHP FastCGI daemon, php70_fpm. Enable them in *etc/rc.conf.local* along with httpd.

```
httpd_flags=""
pkg_scripts="mysqld php70_fpm"
```

You can now configure MariaDB and PHP

MariaDB Setup

Before you create your first database entry, configure MariaDB to work with httpd.

MariaDB (and MySQL) servers normally communicate with clients through a Unix socket in */var/run/mysql/mysql.sock*. Httpd can only access files in */var/www*, however. This blocks PHP programs on the site from talking to your database. The easiest way around this is to move the MariaDB socket into the chroot.[12]

```
# mkdir -p /var/www/var/run/mysql
# chown _mysql:_mysql /var/www/var/run/mysql
```

MariaDB has a directory to put the socket in. Tell the server and the client about it by editing */etc/my.cnf*. You must make matching entries under both [client] and [mysqld].

```
[client]
socket = /var/www/var/run/mysql/mysql.sock
[mysqld]
socket = /var/www/var/run/mysql/mysql.sock
```

If you have trouble at any later part of the installation process, verify your MySQL socket path.

Before you can create your Wordpress database, you need a basic MySQL database with tables to record users, the existence of databases, and so on. Run mysql_install_db(1) to perform this basic setup, then fire up the database.

```
# mysql_install_db
# rcctl start mysqld
```

A default MySQL database requires no authentication and includes a variety of well-known test data. Assign a root access password and toss out the cruft by running mysql_secure_installation(1). Remember, just because MySQL and Unix both have a thing called "the root

---

12   You can do this in one command with install(1), but that would require I explain it, and I can't be bothered.

password," they don't have to be the *same* root password. Use different passwords.

Each Wordpress installation needs a database user and its own private database. Yes, Wordpress pros say you can run any number of sites with a single database and one user. You're in enough trouble here, so start small. The process for creating a Wordpress database and user has been pretty consistent for many years, so we'll cover it here. Log into your MySQL database.

```
# mysql -u root -p
```

Enter the database's root password when prompted.

Your Wordpress database needs a username, a password, and a database. I'm using **wpuser**, wppwd, and wpdb for this example, but you need to pick more unique names. The user only needs to enter these once, so make them as deliciously complicated as you like.

```
> create database wpdb;
Query OK, 1 row affected (0.06 sec)
> grant all privileges on wpdb.* to \
  "wpuser"@"localhost" identified by "wppwd";
Query OK, 0 rows affected (0.01 sec)
> flush privileges;
Query OK, 0 rows affected (0.01 sec)
> quit
```

After creating the database and user, set up PHP.

Configuring PHP

OpenBSD has a separate configuration file and modules directory for each version of PHP. As I'm running PHP 7.0, the configuration is in /etc/php-7.0.ini. The default is fine for most Wordpress installs, but if you need to turn on debugging, increase the stack size, or perform other PHP configuration, look there.

OpenBSD doesn't activate each module when it's installed. Instead, each module needs its own initiation file. Packages install example initiation files in a sample directory. To activate them, copy them to the configuration directory for that version of PHP. The configuration directory for PHP 7.0 is /etc/php-7.0, and the examples appear in /etc/php-7.0.sample. I installed the modules needed by Wordpress, so I must activate everything.

```
# cd /etc/php-7.0
# cp ../php-7.0.sample/* .
```

That should take care of PHP itself. But we also need the PHP-FPM engine. We enabled it in /etc/rc.conf.local, but you still need to start it.

```
# rcctl start php70_fpm
```

While PHP-FPM should run fine as is, if you find you need special configuration you can adjust /etc/php-fpm.conf.

If you're writing your own PHP software, you should know that PHP 7 has a module to interface to OpenBSD's pledge(2). The PHP-pledge project (https://github.com/tvlooy/php-pledge) is experimental as I write this, but you should certainly investigate it for your own projects.

Alternate FastCGI Sockets

PHP needs to run through PHP-FPM, not via slowcgi. You need to tell httpd to use a different FastCGI socket for files ending in .php.

```
server "blog.mallard.info" {
   listen on * port 80
   directory index index.php
   location "*.php" {
     fastcgi socket "/run/php-fpm.sock"
   }
}
```

We again assume that you're making /var/www/htdocs the server's root directory. If you use another root directory, define it with a root statement.

The critical parts here happen in the location statement. Any file that ends in .php gets passed through to the FastCGI socket. We want to use the PHP-FPM socket, not the default slowcgi(8) socket, so we specify that socket by path.

Reboot your server somewhere about now. Make sure that httpd, MariaDB, and PHP-FPM all restart after a boot. Fix any problems before proceeding.

Installing Wordpress

Once the operating system and supporting applications are configured, take a run at Wordpress and the chroot.

Wordpress must be able to resolve hostnames, and it needs access to the local time. Create /var/www/etc and copy (not symlink!) /etc/hosts, /etc/resolv.conf, and /etc/localtime into this directory.

Move the default /var/www/htdocs out of the way. You don't need any of the files in it. You'll create a new htdocs instead. Grab the latest Wordpress tarball, extract it, and rename the new wordpress directory to htdocs. Make this directory and everything in it owned by the httpd user, www.

```
# ftp https://wordpress.org/latest.tar.gz
# tar -xzf latest.tar.gz
# mv wordpress htdocs
# chown -R www:www htdocs
```

Browse to your site. You should see the Wordpress installation screen. You can now walk through the install routine and bring up your site.

If you can bring Wordpress up, you can do anything. Let's proceed to TLS.

Chapter 6: Transport Layer Security

Transport Layer Security, or TLS, is a key component of web security. It's the successor to Secure Sockets Layer, or SSL. TLS is the thing that puts the green padlock in your users' web browsers to tell them that a site is secure.

TLS and SSL are similar but not interoperable. Additionally, SSL's security protections have been broken. The US government forbids even the most recent version, SSL 3.0, from use in health care or sensitive documents. Standards bodies like PCI disallow SSL for financial transactions. Traffic protected by any version of SSL (or even the first version of TLS, 1.0) is vulnerable to decryption and alteration. Some sites still offer SSL, mostly to support old browsers. Additionally, you'll find people using the term SSL when they mean TLS. Much like "class C network," the term "SSL" is going to stick around for decades after it's become irrelevant. It even endures in file paths. File paths are forever.

The LibreSSL library underlying httpd does not support any version of SSL.[13] You literally cannot create a site that uses the SSL protocol with LibreSSL. LibreSSL does support all current versions of TLS.

The presence of TLS on a web site doesn't make the site secure any more than the presence of a padlock in a garden shed secures the shed. But properly configured and applied, TLS secures web transactions against certain types of snooping, spoofing, and traffic alteration.

---

13   Yes, the library's name includes SSL, but it doesn't do SSL. The irony does not escape… anyone, really.

TLS is a hierarchical mechanism based on cryptographic certificates. Each TLS client, such as a browser or a mail server, has a list of trusted certificate-signing agencies. These "certificate authorities" issue digitally signed TLS certificates to web sites. When a TLS client encounters a certificate, it compares the signature on that certificate to its list of ultimately trusted certificates. If the certificate is signed by one of those agencies, the certificate is trusted and the friendly little "lock" icon shows up in the user's browser. If the certificate is not signed by one of those trusted certificate authorities, the browser flashes dire threats to you and your loved ones.

How TLS Works

Common understanding is that TLS makes a web site "secure." Common understanding is wrong. Let's see what TLS does, and then what it doesn't do.

What TLS Does

TLS verifies control of a domain name and protects data in transit.

A certificate authority is supposed to verify that the site that claimsto be a domain really is that domain. If my web server claims to be openbsd.org but is really mallard.info, TLS should warn the user that the site is bogus. If a malicious network engineer has redirected Amazon's web site to his proxy so he can intercept your credit card numbers and login credentials, TLS should throw up its warning message.

Data exchanged over a TLS-protected network connection is secure from someone who can sniff the connection. TLS protects information like usernames and passwords in transit so they remain confidential and unchanged. It does nothing to ensure that the data actually arrives—that's the responsibility of lower network layers—but any data that makes it across the connection is correct.

That is everything that TLS does for you.

For certificate authorities, TLS generates a revenue stream in exchange for running scripts.

What TLS Doesn't Do

TLS is not Magic Security Fairy Dust. It provides no special protection against intruders. A malicious hacker can aim his tools at a poorly designed web site wrapped in TLS and rip it open just as easily as he could a non-TLS version.

TLS does not verify identity. It does verify who controls a domain, but it doesn't verify that the domain is what it claims to be. A TLS certificate is no guarantee that the person who controls the domain michaelwlucastheauthor.com is actually "Michael W Lucas, the author." It only guarantees that the client has established a connection with a server with that domain name.

Some certificate authorities offer Extended Validation (or EV) certificates. These purport to verify the identity of the server's owner. Most TLS clients only make this information available if the user chooses to dig for it. Computers don't care about human identity, after all; they concern themselves only with the domain name.

TLS Organizational Problems

Certificate authorities are organizations built by humans, and have human problems.

Many certificate authorities that offer extended validation have a really iffy record when it comes to actually validating identity. People have gotten bogus certificates issued for large sites such as Google and Microsoft. We know about some of these bogus certificates because the person who got the certificate notified the press. We don't know about the people who got bogus certificates and kept their mouths shut. Certificate authorities are not interested in broadcasting their failures, even when they notice one.

Additionally, getting a certificate signed costs money. Less expensive CAs charge a few dollars, while EV certificates can cost tens of thousands of dollars.

Money changes how organizations work. Organizations work to protect their revenue streams. The existing certificate authorities have at times been referred to as a cabal.

Organizations and even applications can become their own certificate authority. Every Microsoft Windows domain has an internal certificate authority used to authenticate domain requests. This CA isn't usable for other traffic, however.

Some organizations run their own internal CAs. They create a signing certificate and tell all of their clients to trust that certificate. TLS works fine once you get that private certificate installed in all of your client machines, but that certificate cannot interoperate with the outside world.

Many individuals and small organizations use self-signed certificates. These protect traffic from tampering in transit, and most clients can differentiate between "self-signed certificate for this domain" and "self-signed certificate for some other domain." Self-signed certificates always generate an error at the client, however, because no recognized certificate authority has signed them. Average users have been trained that these warnings are a symptom of an untrustworthy site, rather than a sign of partial protection.

Additionally, TLS certificates have an expiration date. Forget to renew the certificate, and clients get more ugly warnings. Yes, the warning message differs, but users don't actually read the message. They'll just assume you've been hacked, because that's what happens on the Internet. Automatic certificate renewal helps, but most CAs make automation less than convenient for small-to-medium organizations.

Various efforts have been made to improve or replace certificate authorities. At one point I hoped that DNS-based Authentication of Named Entities, or DANE, would finally offer a real alternative to CAs. (See my book *DNSSEC Mastery* [Tilted Windmill Press, 2013] for information on using DANE.) It still might, but it hasn't yet.

For today, we live with certificate authorities dominating TLS.

Sysadmins and TLS

When a server needs a TLS certificate, the sysadmin creates a certificate request. The certificate request has three parts: a public key, a private key, and the actual certificate request. You send the certificate request and a chunk of money to a certificate authority. The certificate authority (supposedly) verifies that the requester controls the domain, digitally signs the certificate request with their digital certificate, and returns the signed certificate to you.

A server needs access to both the certificate and the private key file to serve TLS pages. The private key file is highly confidential. Anyone who has that private key file can pretend to be your organization.

Realistically, a certificate request generates a whole bunch of random numbers and attaches one or more hostnames to it. This kind of process is highly amenable to automation.

In the meantime, Let's Encrypt is the best solution we have.

Let's Encrypt

Let's Encrypt (https://letsencrypt.org), or LE, is a fully automated and free certificate authority. The automation isn't only on the certificate authority side; the only way you can get a certificate signed by LE is if the client is automated. You can't paste a certificate request into a browser form: LE is only accessible via special URLs that are nearly unreadable by humans but perfectly palatable to machines. The whole process runs via the Automatic Certificate Management Environment (ACME) protocol.

A Let's Encrypt certificate is only good for 90 days. LE expects that your renewal facilities are also automated, and that you have obliterated the human element from certificate management. LE does not offer Extended Validation certificates, but nobody checks that information anyway, so that's fine.

In short, Let's Encrypt removes much of the systems administration pain of TLS certificates, in exchange for you actually automating your certificate renewal process. You know you should automate this anyway, so it's a win all around.

How does LE do all this for free? They're a 501(c)(3) foundation run by the non-profit Internet Security Research Group, started with help from the Linux Foundation. If you take advantage of their service and have money, send them some.

Httpd includes acme-client(1) for managing LE certificates. While it's installed as part of the web server, you can use these certificates for any application that can use TLS certificates.

The ACME Protocol

How does ACME work? You can find great documents on the protocol's innards at the Let's Encrypt site, but here's an overview.

The first time you fire up an ACME client, the client generates an account key for itself. The client provides the account key's public key to LE, but keeps the private key secret. ACME signs all communication with the LE servers with this keypair.

The client asks LE what it needs to do to verify that it controls the domain it wants a certificate for. LE responds with a list of proof it will accept. These proofs require changes to the domain: perhaps a new DNS record in the domain's zone, or making a signed response available in a particular hidden directory on the domain's web site.

The client chooses which challenge to accept. Once it's completed the challenge by creating the DNS record or changing the host's site, it notifies LE that it can now validate the client's response. Once LE verifies that the change has occurred and is signed with the client's private key, LE allows that keypair to manage that domain.

From that point on, the client can send certificate requests and revocations signed with its key. Let's Encrypt validates the signatures and creates the certificates.

This protocol also means that ACME can only manage public domains. You cannot use LE for private domains like .local, as those domains are deliberately hidden from the global network. You can build a private CA for your hidden domains, however.

Many people rely on Let's Encrypt. Almost all of them schedule certificate maintenance. Many of them schedule these updates on the hour. When you finish your automation and you're ready to put it in cron(8), use a random time.

Let's Encrypt offers two services, production and staging. The production environment limits how many ACME operations you can perform per server. Those limits are high, but if you have heavily loaded servers you should check them before deploying. The staging environment allows an unlimited number of ACME operations, but the certificate is not globally valid. You can download the staging certificate from Let's Encrypt.

Test everything, particularly your first certificates, against Let's Encrypt's staging environment. Once it works, move to production.

Each ACME service needs an account key. The client creates the account key before connecting to the service. You can create a new account key at any time, but a new key cannot revoke existing certificates.

acme-client

The acme-client(1) program lets you create, renew, and manage certificates through the ACME protocol. At this time, the only ACME certification authority is Let's Encrypt.[14]

While ACME supports many challenge types, `acme-client` responds to LE challenges only over HTTP and HTTPS. You can use acme-client only on publicly accessible web servers. Many ACME clients have this same limitation, as many sites lack the dynamic DNS infrastructure to respond easily to ACME challenges.

Unlike many other clients, however, `acme-client` is very simple to use. After some basic httpd configuration so that `acme-client` can make challenge responses available, it Just Works.

Configuring httpd for ACME

Web-based ACME responses all go in the site directory /.well-known/acme-challenge/. That is, an ACME challenge response for mallard.info needs to be available under http://mallard.info/.well-known/acme-challenge/. Each individual ACME challenge sets its own location under that directory. Once the challenge is satisfied and the certificate operation is complete, acme-client deletes the challenge file, so the directory is almost always empty.

Httpd's chroot sets aside a directory for ACME challenge responses, `/var/www/acme`, and `acme-client` puts all challenge responses there. Use a location statement to attach this directory to a virtual server.

---

14   If you're looking to change the world, you could set up an ACME-compatible competitor to Let's Encrypt. Monocultures, even monocultures dominated by great software, are toxic.

```
server "www.mallard.info" {
…
  location "/.well-known/acme-challenge/*" {
    root "/acme"
    root strip 2
    directory no auto index
  }
}
```

The location statement is very standard, as is the root statement. But what's this `root strip 2` thing?

A *root strip* statement removes a number of elements from the front of the request path—the $REQUEST_URI variable, or everything after the server name. LE's check for an ACME challenge response will look something like /.well-known/acme-challenge/honketyblatt123. The `strip 2` statement removes /.well-known/ and /acme-challenge/ from the front of the request, and the location statement steers what's left of the request to `/acme` within the chroot.

Don't enable automatic indexing in `/acme`. If the main server allows automatic indexing, disable it here. If you're not sure if the directory mapping works correctly on a server, create a HTML file in `/var/www/acme` and see if you can call it up in your browser.

Once httpd is configured, you're ready to create your first Let's Encrypt certificate.

acme-client Bootstrap Concerns

Once your web site has TLS, it can securely exchange certificate information with Let's Encrypt. But a site first starting with LE doesn't have a TLS-protected web site. The challenge responses are in plain old unencrypted HTTP. Doesn't that present a man-in-the-middle attack risk?

While someone could intercept your challenge responses, those responses are valueless to an attacker. Each response can only be used once. Each response is digitally signed with the account key. If an intruder can do this, they have demonstrated that they control the domain.

While the client server does not yet have TLS, the Let's Encrypt server certainly does. The client downloads all sensitive information over that TLS connection.

/etc/acme-client.conf

Each domain needs a configuration in `/etc/acme-client.conf`. You can also configure additional ACME services here. While the only ACME service today is Let's Encrypt, that will hopefully change.

Global ACME Configuration

As with so many OpenBSD configuration files, `acme-client.conf` starts with macros. Here's a couple I find useful.

```
le="letsencrypt"
ls="letsencrypt-staging"
```

We'll use these macros throughout the configuration.

We then define ACME authorities. OpenBSD includes the Let's Encrypt production and staging environments by default, so you shouldn't need to edit them, but let's take a quick look.

```
authority letsencrypt {
    agreement url \
        "https://letsencrypt.org/documents/LE-SA-v1.1.1-August-1-2016.pdf"
    api url "https://acme-v01.api.letsencrypt.org/directory"
    account key "/etc/acme/letsencrypt-privkey.pem"
}
```

Here we define the authority *letsencrypt*. We give the URL of the terms of service agreement we've accepted. Should Let's Encrypt change their ToS, or decide to no longer accept this agreement, we'll need to update our config file to point at the new acceptable ToS—or, alternately, reject the ToS and stop using Let's Encrypt.

The API URL is the site we communicate with over ACME.

The account key is the private key for our account. The acme-client(1) program uses this key to uniquely identify this server.

The default configuration includes a similar entry for the Let's Encrypt staging environment. Defining macros for each lets you easily test your configuration against the staging environment. Once you know it works, changing the macro lets you easily switch to production.

Now configure each domain's certificate.

Domain ACME Configuration

Each domain name that you want to use ACME for needs a separate configuration in /etc/acme-client.conf. Here's an example for my domain www.mallard.info.

```
domain www.mallard.info {
    alternative names { mallard.info tarpit.mallard.info }
    domain key "/etc/ssl/acme/mallard/mallard.key"
    domain certificate "/etc/ssl/acme/mallard/mallard.crt"
    domain chain certificate \
        "/etc/ssl/acme/mallard/mallard.chain.pem"
    domain full chain certificate \
        "/etc/ssl/acme/mallard/mallard.fullchain.pem"
    sign with $le
}
```

Each certificate has a primary hostname attached to it. For this entry, the primary hostname is www.mallard.info. Any additional names go into the first entry, "alternative names," separated by spaces.

Much like any other TLS certificate, your ACME certificate must have a private key file and a certificate file. I put all of my TLS certificates in /etc/ssl, but separate the ACME ones into a subdirectory, then I add another layer of per-host subdirectories. These directories must exist before you can run acme-client. Any organization scheme has its problems, so use whatever makes sense to you; there's no wrong way to shoot yourself in the foot.

Let's Encrypt requests also generate a certificate *chain file*. A chain file contains the signing certificate and any parent certificates needed to attach the signing certificate to trusted global certificate. Certificates from many small CAs also use chain files. Each site needs its own chain file. List the chain file in the site configuration.

You might notice that the key files are not in the httpd chroot. Httpd handles keys with privilege separation. The process running as **root** reads the files and sends the keys to the server processes over socketpair(2). This means that you can reload the daemon and have the keys resent to the clients, rather than restarting.

Finally, define the ACME authority that you'll use to sign this certificate. I defined a macro for the Let's Encrypt servers, because I'm too lazy to type authority names over and over again.

Basic acme-client Use

Once a domain has an entry in */etc/acme-client.conf* you can request a TLS certificate for it.

The first time you use an authority, you must create a key for that authority. Your client uses that key to securely identify itself. Add the -A flag the first time you use an authority.

Before creating a certificate, you must create private and public keys for that certificate. The first time you request a certificate for a host, use -D to create that keypair.

The -D and -A flags only create keys if a key does not already exist. You can use these flags in later commands without causing problems.

Add -v to see some more detail on how acme-client works. A second -v spills out all of the ACME communications details. I'd suggest using -vv and studying the output at least once, for your own edification if nothing else.

```
# acme-client -vvAD www.mallard.info
```

Here I'm creating a certificate for www.mallard.info. The acme-client(1) program looks up the hostname in /etc/acme-client.conf and uses that entry to build its ACME request. It creates the account and domain keys as specified in the configuration file.

Now attach the TLS certificate to the server.

Configuring Httpd for TLS

Enabling TLS on an httpd server requires a new listen statement and telling the server where to find the key.

```
server "www.mallard.info" {
    alias mallard.info
    listen on * port 80
    listen on * tls port 443
    tls certificate "/etc/ssl/acme/mallard/mallard.fullchain.pem"
    tls key "/etc/ssl/acme/private/mallard/mallard.key"
    ...
```

While the first three lines of this configuration are very standard, the last three give the TLS configuration.

The fourth line tells httpd to attach to port 443. We add the *tls* keyword to tell httpd that this port uses TLS. 443 is the standard port for TLS web sites.

The *tls certificate* statement gives the path to the site certificate, including the Let's Encrypt certificate chain. You need the full chain.

Finally, the *tls key* statement gives the full path to the private key.

This configuration creates a site available in both TLS and non-TLS versions. Once you test your TLS site, you probably want to automatically redirect non-TLS connections to the TLS version.

Redirecting non-TLS to TLS

Make migrations to TLS as transparent as possible to users. We use httpd macros and redirects to steer users that request the non-TLS version of a page to the TLS version. This requires two servers with the same name.

```
server "www.mallard.info" {
   listen on * port 80
   block return 301 "https://$SERVER_NAME$REQUEST_URI"
}

server "www.mallard.info" {
   listen on * tls port 443
   tls certificate "/etc/ssl/acme/mallard/fullchain.pem"
   …
```

The first entry is for the version of www.mallard.info that runs on port 80—the non-TLS site. All requests to this site get a permanent redirect to the TLS version. This version doesn't need a root directory or any other settings.

The second entry is the start of the TLS version of the same site. Note the lack of a listen statement for port 80.

HTTP Strict Transport Security

TLS is not perfect. A user might follow an old bookmark or manually type a site name and get to a non-SSL version of a site. Your web designer might screw up and include non-TLS elements in the site. An intruder might attempt to hijack the web site hoping that the end user will tell the browser to ignore the warning and proceed anyway. While redirects to the TLS site can help, redirects can't protect against malice or misconfigurations. If only a web site had a way to tell a browser to be a right bastard and not permit these.

We have *HTTP Strict Transport Security*, or HSTS, for just such situations.

By enabling HSTS, the server tells the client to automatically redirect any non-TLS connections to TLS. The server also tells the client to disable the client's ability to override any certificate errors. While it doesn't protect the client's initial connection to the site, it does protect all subsequent requests.

Enable HSTS in a server with the *hsts* option.

```
server "www.mallard.info" {
  alias "mallard.info"
  listen on * tls port 443
  hsts
  …
```

HSTS requires support in the browser, but modern versions of all popular browsers support it.[15] Browsers lose the HSTS setting when they flush their cache.

Your server now ensures TLS compliance. Until the certificate expires in 90 days, at least.

Maintaining Certificates

Certificates mostly work, until they don't. If you want to keep users from getting those nasty browser warnings, you'll need to renew your certificates before they expire. Certain security problems mean you need to revoke the certificate before it expires. Finally, you'll get best performance if you include an updated notice that the certificate has not been revoked.

Any time you want to work on certificates, though, start with backups.

Backing Up Certificates

Renewing and revoking certificates destroys the old certificate files. If Let's Encrypt certificates are free, why back them up? The short answer is, things happen. I didn't back up my certificates until I started writing this section of the book, when I quickly found myself wishing I had the certificate files I'd just destroyed, for comparison. Whether you back up unused certificates or not depends entirely on your environment.

---

15   We elite Lynx users don't need modern security anyway. We're just wiser that way. The Internet was better without images and ecommerce. Get off my lawn.

Use the -b flag to tell `acme-client` to keep a copy of old certificate files. These backups include the `cert.pem`, `chain.pem`, and `fullchain.pem` files. The old versions of the files are retained in the same directory, but each is renamed with an extension of the time in epochal seconds. You'll find files like `/etc/ssl/acme/chain-1483473110.pem`. Use date(1) to convert these timestamps to human-readable dates.

```
# date -r 1483473110
Tue Jan  3 14:51:50 EST 2017
```

While certificate files are tiny, you should still go in and delete unneeded ones every so often.

For conciseness, the examples herein do not include backing up files. I recommend you do back your files up.

Renewing Certificates

Let's Encrypt recommends renewing their certificates every 60 days. While the certificates expire every 90 days, waiting to renew until the last day is a great way to have a bad day every three months. Let's Encrypt will let you automatically renew certificates within 30 days of expiration.

To update a certificate, run `acme-client` with the certificate's main hostname in `/etc/acme-client.conf`. It's much like the process to issue the certificate. Normally it runs silently, but the first time you try this at the command line or if you need to debug something, add the -v flag for more verbosity.

```
# acme-client -v www.mallard.info
acme-client: /etc/ssl/acme/www/www.crt: certificate
  valid: 77 days left
```

There's no need to renew this certificate yet.

86

To force renewing a certificate early, add the -F flag. Functional automation means never needing to renew early, but every sysadmin knows that the best automation fails only during your well-earned vacation or over the holiday weekend.

The acme-client(1) manual page has a sample renewal script meant to be run from cron(8). Why do you need a whole script to handle renewals? When acme-client renews the certificate, you must tell httpd to reread the file.

```
#!/bin/sh
acme-client www.mallard.info
if [ $? -eq 0 ]
   then
      /etc/rc.d/httpd reload
   fi
```

Modify the script for your domain, run it from cron once a day, and you're done. You could run it less often, but OCSP (later this chapter) requires more frequent checks.

When I first tested automated renewal, I added -v to the acme-client call. Every day, I received a certificate valid email. Once I saw the automation renew the certificate and restart the web server without my intervention, I removed the -v from the script. If your monitoring system identifies certificates within 30 days of expiring, you can rely on that instead. Or, better still, in addition to.

Certificate Revocation

Anyone who has your server's key pair can masquerade as your site. If an intruder can copy the private and public key files, they can set up a server that is indistinguishable from yours. Yes, a successful masquerade requires more than just those files, but the files are a necessary prerequisite.

If you have reason to doubt the sanctity of your key files, ask Let's Encrypt to *revoke* the certificate. Browsers give different scary warnings when encountering a revoked certificate. The user still won't read the warnings, but maybe they'll call the helpdesk and warn your IT department.

While all certificate authorities offer certificate revocation, very few of their customers use that feature. Commercial CAs would like you to revoke compromised certificates, because then you'd need to buy a new certificate immediately. Very few organizations revoke certificates on a mere suspicion, because then they'd have to purchase new certificates. By removing the financial aspect, Let's Encrypt makes mere suspicion a sufficient reason to revoke a certificate. In my book, this feature alone makes me prefer Let's Encrypt.

Revoking the certificate destroys the `cert.pem`, `chain.pem`, and `fullchain.pem` files. If you want to keep the files, add `-b` or make your own copies. Restarting httpd without the key files becomes problematic. Fortunately, the revoked certificate doesn't prevent you from validating new ACME challenges.

While revoking a certificate destroys the certificate files, it does not destroy your private key file (defaulting to `/etc/ssl/acme/private/privkey.pem`). If you believe the key is compromised, move or destroy this file before issuing a new certificate.

Revoke a certificate with the `-r` flag. You can create a new certificate immediately thereafter.

```
# acme-client -br www.mallard.info mallard.info
```

Once you revoke the certificate, browsers immediately get certificate revocation notices. No restart of httpd is needed. Now create your new certificate.

```
# mv /etc/ssl/acme/private/privkey.pem \
  untrusted-privkey.pem
# acme-client -N www.mallard.info mallard.info
# rcctl restart httpd
```

You have deployed a new, unsullied certificate.

Somewhere in here, you really should address the security flaws that compromised your certificate.

Optimizing Revocation Checks with OCSP

Think about revoked certificates for a moment. It's easy for me to declare that the certificate on my host is no good. But what about a stolen copy? If someone has a copy of my private key from before it's revoked, how does the browser know that the certificate is revoked?

The answer is, the browser checks.

Modern web browsers validate every TLS connection with the *Online Certificate Status Protocol*, or OCSP. Each Certificate Authority maintains a list of certificates that have not yet expired but have been revoked. When the client identifies the certificate issuer, it queries one of the CA's *OCSP responders* to determine if the certificate is still valid. The responder says "I haven't revoked this certificate yet," and the browser proceeds.

Yes, OCSP increases network traffic utilization by a minuscule amount. It slows down web sites, as the browser won't approve the certificate until it completes the OCSP query. The older, pre-TLS system required SSL clients to download a complete Certificate Revocation List (CRL) every time they encountered an SSL certificate. CRLs used *far* more bandwidth than OCSP.

TLS is becoming more and more important. Search engines are starting to emphasize sites that use TLS over sites that don't. TLS is no longer only for big sites, but for small ones as well. Even my web sites use TLS, and I'm unknown beyond the itty bitty open source BSD world. Your site's performance is limited to that of your certificate authority's OCSP responder... unless you can bypass it somehow.

As a site administrator, you can improve performance by telling the browser that the certificate is still valid. The web server does this by going to the certificate authority and requesting a signed notice that the certificate is still valid. The web server provides this notice to the client.

Now all you need to do is get the OCSP certificate.

Retrieving an OCSP Certificate

You can retrieve the OCSP certificate from a CA through a nightmarish series of openssl(1) commands. Fortunately, OpenBSD includes an OCSP fetcher, ocspcheck(8). As Let's Encrypt doesn't support OCSP nonces, use -N to disable requesting one. Use -o to tell ocspcheck where to put the created file. OCSP certificates traditionally end in .der. Use the full certificate chain file as the last argument. The first time you run ocspcheck, add a -v to get more detail about what it does. Here I get an OCSP cert for my host www.mallard.info.

```
# cd /etc/ssl/acme/www
# ocspcheck -No www.der www.fullchain.pem
```

You should now have a OCSP cert in www.der.

OCSP and Httpd

Attach the OCSP certificate to the web site.

```
server "www.mallard.info" {
  ...
  tls certificate "/etc/ssl/acme/www/www.fullchain.pem"
  tls key "/etc/ssl/acme/www/www.key"
  tls ocsp "/etc/ssl/acme/www/www.der"
  ...
}
```

Restart httpd, and you'll have OCSP working.

Verify OCSP

Most browsers don't display OCSP certificates in the SSL certificate information. How can you be sure it's working?

How can you verify OCSP? Most people need an OpenSSL command, but OpenBSD users can use their TLS-aware nc(1). It's not as simple as connecting to port 443, though. You must provide additional information for the host find the proper certificate.

```
$ printf "GET / HTTP/1.1\r\nHost: site\r\nConnection:
close\r\n\r\n" | nc -ce site -T muststaple host 443
```

Here's how I'd test the OCSP stapling on www.mallard.info.

```
$ printf "GET / HTTP/1.1\r\nHost: www.mallard.info\r
\nConnection: close \r\n\r\n" | nc -ce www.mallard.info
-T muststaple www.mallard.info 443
```

If you get an error like

```
nc: tls handshake failed (no stapled OCSP response provided),
```

OCSP stapling is misconfigured. If you get the HTML code for the server's front page, the site response included OCSP. Congratulations, you're among the TLS elite!

Until your certificates expire, that is.

Certificate Maintenance

OCSP certificates expire after a week. The easiest way to maintain them automatically is in the same daily script that maintains your SSL certificate.

```
acme-client -v www.mallard.info
ocspcheck -vN -o /etc/ssl/acme/mallard/mallard.der \
  /etc/ssl/acme/mallard/mallard.fullchain.pem
if [ $? == 0 ];
  then
    /etc/rc.d/httpd reload
  fi
```

Have cron(8) to run this every day at a random time. It will check your TLS and OCSP certificates, update them, and reload httpd if needed.

Tuning TLS

For most of us, httpd's TLS works. It supports the latest security protocols and encryption algorithms, and disables less secure and deprecated ones.

Sadly, not everybody else is as up to date.

We've all experienced that critical customer or business partner who is utterly indifferent to their obsolete equipment and software. I know of more than one company still critically dependent on Internet Explorer 6, which barely supports TLS 1.0. If such an organization gives you enough money, you'll want to interoperate with their systems. Httpd defaults to only offering TLS 1.2, but you can enable older protocols. Similarly, you might need outdated and less secure encryption and hashing algorithms.

Httpd lets you tune certain TLS characteristics—not all the way down to nothing, but pretty far down. In almost all cases, adjusting TLS settings is poor practice and reduces cryptographic security. Leave the defaults in place unless you have a very specific, operations-driven reason to change them. If you must change them, address the operational concern that drove you to change them and return httpd to its default settings.

TLS Versions

TLS 1.2, httpd's default, is several years old and well-supported by all modern browsers and clients. When a client that doesn't support TLS 1.2 connects to an httpd-backed site, it disconnects itself. The user sees nothing.

The *tls protocols* option lets you choose to support older TLS versions. Give this on a per-server basis. The current list of protocols is available in LibreSSL's tls_config_parse_protocols(3) manual page, but here are the protocols supported as of OpenBSD 6.1.

The *default* setting means to support TLS 1.2 only. Yes, this is the default, but you could choose to explicitly state it.

```
tls protocol default
```

To offer all TLS versions supported by your version of LibreSSL, use the *all* option.

```
tls protocols all
```

Suppose the client can only handle TLS versions 1.0 or 1.1, and that exposure to version 1.2 makes terrible things happen. And suppose that letting terrible things happen is, sadly, not an option. You can also specify specific protocols, separating them by commas or colons. If you use commas, you must quote the entire protocol list.

```
tls protocols tlsv1.0:tlsv1.1
```

Check tls_config_parse_protocols for the current list of TLS versions.

You can also exclude a protocol from a list by putting an exclamation point in front of it. Here we support everything LibreSSL offers, except TLS 1.2. Because some business partner hates all that is good and decent.

```
tls protocols "all,!tlsv1.2"
```

If you need to tweak the TLS protocols list, fix the problem that means you need to tweak the protocols list.

TLS Ciphers

You can set the list of ciphers, or cryptographic algorithms, a virtual server will offer. Like TLS versions, the ciphers LibreSSL offers are chosen for a reason. Don't change them without a good reason. If you have a good reason, get rid of the reason. We won't cover all of the cipher options, only the ones you're most likely to encounter in the real world.

Web servers and clients each support a variety of cryptographic algorithms. At the beginning of a TLS connection, the two negotiate their preferred algorithm. The openssl(1) manual page gives list of supported ciphers, under CIPHERS. You can view the list with the `openssl ciphers` command. Add `-v` for more detail, and `-v` for even more detail. Ciphers have names that describe the algorithms they use, like ECDHE-ECDSA-AES256-SHA. Web server sysadmins don't need to know how the names are built or how the algorithms work internally, only to recognize such names when they appear.

The most common reason to adjust the list of ciphers is to remove an algorithm. If someone finds a flaw in a cryptographic algorithm or its implementation, you might want to turn that algorithm off on your site until LibreSSL is patched to address the flaw. Fortunately, this is straightforward.

LibreSSL includes several named sets of ciphers. The most common is DEFAULT, the list of algorithms most commonly used. Some groups are defined by the key's length, such as LOW for 54-bit and 64-bit keys, MEDIUM for 128-bit keys, and HIGH for keys longer than 128 bits. Others are defined by the algorithm family, such as 3DES and RC4 and MD5. Then there's groups like ALL, that contain most (but not all) supported algorithms. Read the manual page for the details on each of these. Right now, it's DEFAULT that concerns us.

Use the *tls ciphers* option to set a server's cryptographic algorithm in `httpd.conf`. Start with the DEFAULT list. Add more ciphers to the acceptable list by separating them with colons or commas. Exclude ciphers from a list by putting an exclamation point in front of them. Here we turn off the ECDHE-RSA-AES256-SHA cipher.

```
tls ciphers "DEFAULT,!ECDHE-RSA-AES256-SHA"
```

You can exclude one list from another. Here we tell the server to use every cipher, except those that use RC4.

```
tls ciphers "DEFAULT,!RC4"
```

You must set ciphers on a per-server basis. Sysadmins with hosts that support many servers will find include files useful for broad changes.

You can also build completely custom lists of ciphers for your httpd installation. For most of us, this is a really, really bad idea. You can set Diffie-Hellman parameters and elliptic curves. If you think building custom cipher lists is a good idea, you're wrong.

TLS 1.3

TLS 1.3 is the newest version of TLS, and is just starting to appear out in the world. LibreSSL does not support TLS 1.3 as I write this, but support is expected to appear before long. Once it appears, you can configure it much like the other TLS versions.

TLS 1.3 drops support for quite a few old and less secure algorithms, however. There should be no need to tune it at all.

Your web transport is now as secure as it can be and still run on the Internet. Let's look at a couple final tidbits about httpd.

Chapter 7: Httpd Odds and Ends

While httpd normally performs well, a high-load site might require additional tuning. You can also adjust certain performance characteristics on a per-server basis.

Performance

Httpd has only one global performance setting, *prefork*. Each httpd process handles one incoming request at a time. A busy server needs more processes. With prefork, you tell httpd how many servers to start. The default is 3.

```
prefork 6
```

How many httpd processes can you run? That has nothing to do with httpd and everything to do with the amount of load your system can handle. Try some load testing on your equipment and find out.

TCP/IP Tuning

OpenBSD's TCP/IP stack has been adjusted to handle almost any network conditions. Most hosts require no network tuning. On very rare occasions, though, a sysadmin might have to use sysctl(8) to adjust the operating system instance's IP stack. This is highly rare.

On even rarer occasions, a virtual server might need specific TCP/IP tuning. Httpd allows you to do this. For almost all of us, this is a truly terrible idea that will cause no end of suffering.[16] That fraction of a percent of you who need this feature will find it invaluable. Use the *tcp* option to adjust the network's behavior for a virtual server.

---

16   If you want to cause yourself pain, though, who am I to say no?

If you don't understand how a TCP change affects the system, don't try it.

The *tcp backlog* option lets you set how many connections for this host can be pending at a time. It defaults to 10. The kernel accepts 10 connection requests for each httpd process and puts them on hold until the process is ready for them. If all your httpd processes have full queues you need either more processes, deeper queues, or a less popular web site. The `kern.somaxconn` sysctl sets the maximum value you can use here, normally 128. Unless you have a simple web site where each request gets served really quickly, you're better off increasing the number of server processes than upping the backlog.

```
tcp backlog 128
```

Clever jerks have figured out how to use the Time To Live (TTL) of IP packets to attack routers. Httpd can automatically discard IP packets that have a TTL below a given value, as described by the Generalized TTL Security Mechanism (GTSM, or RFC 5082). If you need to deploy GTSM on your web server, you can.

```
tcp ip minttl 255
```

You can manually set the IP TTL on httpd responses. You'd normally do this to hack around malfunctioning equipment. You might also do it to limit how far a host can send responses. A TTL of 2 means that your web site is visible only on the local LAN and one network away. A firewall is the sensible place to enforce this kind of security policy, but presumably you have your reasons for doing it here.[17]

```
tcp ip ttl 2
```

---

17   My guess would be "because the firewall administrator is a jerk," but it's possibly another reason. Possibly.

TCP has a variety of congestion control and packet loss control mechanisms. In some cases, these mechanisms reduce performance. You might try either the TCP_NODELAY option, the TCP_SACK option, or both to see if performance improves for the majority of your clients. The tcp(4) man page discusses both of these options.

```
tcp nodelay
tcp sack
```

The TCP window size is a critical part of a network stack's performance. OpenBSD adjusts window size as needed, and you should almost never need to set it manually. In those rare cases, you can nail the window size to a specific setting with the tcp ip socket buffer setting. Here I set the window size to 256K.

```
tcp socket buffer 262144
```

For the most part, though, leave all of these settings alone.

PF Maximum States

PF's state table defaults to only supporting a maximum of 10,000 entries. This means that if you have 10,000 current TCP sessions, the host won't accept any more connections. The state table includes sessions that haven't timed out yet, and some clients open a daft number of TCP/IP connections for a single request, so this doesn't mean 10,000 current httpd sessions.

To see the current number of state table entries, use pfctl(8).

```
# pfctl -ss | wc -l
5791
```

This web server isn't overloaded, and it's already at half the limit. Better increase it. Use the set limit states option in *pf.conf* to raise the maximum.

```
set limit states 20000
```

Don't just raise this limit willy-nilly, as state table memory is pre-allocated. It's not a lot of memory, mind you, but if you wanted to pointlessly sacrifice memory you'd run a different application.

User Managed Web Sites

Sometimes you have a web site maintained by a user. Maybe you offer them other services, like a database, but you hand all responsibility for the site's files and content off to the user. This is common in hosting organizations.

Such users need to be able to access their own files, and only their own files. They shouldn't go wandering around into other customers' stuff, even with read-only permissions. The sysadmin needs to lock such users in a cage and keep them there. Most of this configuration happens in the SSH server, but you'll also need some basic systems administration and minor httpd tweaks.

While you can put several web sites under one account, I habitually tie each web site to a unique account. This gives me freedom to move sites between servers as needed. That's the model I'll use here for mallard.info, a site maintained by Bill the web developer.

First, the user needs a home directory. This home directory should be on a partition mounted nodev and nosuid, like _/var/www_ defaults to. If you need suid programs in _/var/www_, I'd suggest you create a new partition only for these users and mount it under _/var/www_. I'm putting all of my external users in _/var/www/users_.

Now you need a system group for these users. Give it a suitable name.

```
# groupadd -v vermin
```

These users don't need very many resources at all, so feel free to reduce the group's limits in _/etc/login.conf_.

We need sshd(8) to chroot any user in this group into their home directory. Add the following to the end of */etc/ssh/sshd_config*.

```
Match group vermin
  ChrootDirectory %h
  ForceCommand internal-sftp
  AllowTcpForwarding no
```

Create a user. Give them a shell of */sbin/nologin*, and add them to your sftp-only group. Put their home directory under */var/www/users*. I could call the user bill, after site maintainer Bill, but then I'd have to remember which user goes with which site, and I'd rather inconvenience Bill than myself. I call the first user **mallard**, after his domain mallard.info, and put his home directory in */var/www/users/mallard*.

Create two subdirectories in the user's home directory, *www* and *logs*. The *www* directory will contain the user's web files. The *logs* directory has their logs.

Log handling is slightly tricky. Httpd doesn't allow you to define per-site log directories outside the main log directory. Use a symlink to attach the user's log directory to httpd's defined structure. As a user can't follow a symlink out of a chroot, but httpd can follow symlinks, you must link the site log directory to the user's home directory.

```
# ln -s /var/www/users/mallard/logs /var/www/logs/mallard
```

Now tell httpd about this site.

```
server "www.mallard.info" {
  ...
  root "/users/mallard/www"
  log access "mallard/mallard_access"
  log error "mallard/mallard_err"
}
```

Restart httpd. Once you test your user's access and verify that files uploaded to the site directory appear on the web, all you can do is sit back and wait for Bill's inevitable phone call lamenting that FTP and SFTP are different things.

Now that you have a working web site, let's make it redundant.

Chapter 8: Common Address Redundancy Protocol

Every host needs patching and hardware maintenance. No matter how hard you work to keep a system up, at some time it's going to need downtime. Can your organization handle having its web site down after hours for maintenance? Or is the web site a key part of its business, making downtime unacceptable?

One solution for keeping a service like HTTP available at all times is the *Common Address Redundancy Protocol*, or *CARP*. Like the similar protocols, CARP is intended for a situation where you have multiple hosts on the same network segment offering the same service, such as a web site.

The trick with CARP is that the service is tied to one or more IP addresses that are not permanently attached to any single host. It's often called a *floating address*. Each host has an entirely different IP address for management. CARP temporarily attaches the service address to one of the hosts. When that host dies, the CARP protocol on the other hosts notice. One of the other hosts picks up the address and offers the service. The host holding the floating address is called the *CARP master*, while the others is a *CARP backup*.

CARP cannot transparently switch active TCP session termination from one host to another. (It can pass state on firewalls via pfsync(8), but that's a separate thing.) If you're serving large files off on your web site, the client will notice the interruption. Most clients can create a new connection and pick up where they left off, though.

If you're familiar with either Virtual Router Redundancy Protocol (VRRP) or Hot Standby Router Protocol (HSRP), CARP will feel very familiar. CARP has stronger authentication and integrity checks than either of those protocols, however.

CARP Hosts

Start with two identical hosts. They don't have to be identical, of course, but identical hardware will save you trouble over the years they'll be in service. Wire both of them into the same network segment.

Once the hosts are physically identical, install them identically. Use the same version of OpenBSD. Use the same partitioning. Install the same packages. If you have a configuration management system such as Ansible, use it. If you don't have a configuration management system, change the hosts at the same time. [18] Spend the extra time to make things correct from the beginning.

Each host needs identical packet filter rules. The PF rules discussed in Chapter 9 are a decent place to start. CARP is TCP/IP protocol number 112—no, not port 112, protocol 112, just like TCP is protocol 6 and UDP is protocol 17. You'll need a PF rule to pass CARP traffic on each interface, with a rule like this near the top. Use `no state` to prevent CARP from synchronizing its state through pfsync(8).

```
pass in quick proto carp no state
```

Time spent configuring your hosts properly before they go live will save you boundless trouble later.

CARP Prerequisites

On each host, identify the network interface that's attached to the shared network segment—especially if the host has multiple interfaces.

---

18   And, if you don't have a configuration management system: get one. Even if you think you don't need it, you need it.

Each redundancy group needs an authentication password. This password will appear in clear text in the system configuration files, so don't reuse an existing password.

You might want one host to be the master when available, and the others to serve only when the preferred master is unavailable. Sometimes it's because the backup hardware has less capacity than the preferred master, while other times it's just because you like knowing where things are. Decide if you care, and if so, which host is the master and which is the backup.

Finally, assign an IP address to the redundancy group.

What's a redundancy group? I'm glad you asked.

Redundancy Groups and Network Mayhem

A group of hosts supporting the same IP addresses is called a *redundancy group*. Each redundancy group on a network segment needs its own *virtual host ID*, or VHID. The VHID is an eight-bit number used within CARP to distinguish one redundancy group from another. Each VHID on a network segment must be unique.

Here's where things get a little tricky, though. CARP, VRRP, and HSRP are all similar protocols. They all have something like redundancy groups and VHIDs. The language changes, but they all perform similar functions and work in a roughly analogous manner. Only the little details of protocol, configuration, and implementation differ.

Not all vendors implement their protocols well. They might expect that their failover protocol is the only one on the network. If your router speaks VRRP, what will it do when it sees a CARP packet? Most of the time, it's fine. For certain vendors, running certain software versions, the answer is some variant of "crash and die." Maybe the router CPU starts running at 100% and stays there, or a switch transforms into a hub and broadcasts everything everywhere. Multiple people have reported that even when using different redundancy protocols, having identical VHIDs on the same network causes issues.

Before deploying CARP, talk to your network team and other folks who have servers on the same network segment. Find out if they're already using any redundancy protocols such as CARP, VRRP, or HSRP. If they are, find out which VHIDs are free and use those. Taking a few minutes to say, "the network team already uses 1 to 99, the server team gets 100 to 199, the rest is for anyone who comes along later," can save you massive headaches later. There's plenty of space to avoid each other's VHIDs.[19]

If they're different protocols, why does separating VHIDs matter? The protocols have different packet formats, but VRRP and CARP put the VHID in the same place. A VRRP cluster that sees a CARP packet can check the VHID and correctly identify it as "not my problem."

Now let's configure one of these groups.

A Two-Server CARP

I have two web servers, www1 at 192.0.2.101/24 and www2 at 192.0.2.102/24. Both servers have a single network interface, em0. I want to use CARP to provide the floating address of 192.0.2.100/24. The password will be *PetRats*, because the command line is long and the print version of this book is narrow. I'm using VHID 89, because most examples use boring old VHID 1.

Create a CARP interface on both hosts. As I'm using VHID 89, I'll call this interface carp89.

```
# ifconfig carp89 create
```

If you have a preferred master and a preferred backup host, you must tell each host to allow CARP *preemption*. Preemption is where

---

19   Reduce the odds of having to speak to another human being by setting your packet sniffer to look for protocol 112.

a CARP host can tell the current master "I have higher priority, hand over the IP." Set the sysctl `net.inet.carp.preempt` to 1 to enable preemption.

```
# sysctl net.inet.carp.preempt=1
net.inet.carp.preempt: 0 -> 1
```

To have this persist after a reboot, add it to *`/etc/sysctl.conf`* as well.

CARP uses *advertising skew*, or *advskew* entry, to control how a host advertises itself to its redundancy group. Higher skews indicate a lower priority. Other hosts in the redundancy group can declare themselves more important and claim the address. You'll need to set an advskew to make a host a preferred backup.

Start by configuring the preferred backup. Even if you don't have a preferred backup, I explain some bits about CARP in that section, so don't skip ahead. Sorry.

Configuring the Assigned Backup

Use ifconfig(8) to configure CARP, like so.

```
# ifconfig interface vhid vhidnumber pass password \
    carpdev interface advskew 100 ip netmask mask
```

Our CARP interface is carp89. The VHID is 89. Our pre-chosen password is PetRats. The physical interface underlying this is em0. Assign an advskew of 100 to make this host declare itself less important than others. Let's attach this CARP interface to a physical interface, give it an IP address, and tell it to be the backup.

```
# ifconfig carp89 vhid 89 pass PetRats carpdev em0 \
    advskew 100 192.0.2.100 netmask 255.255.255.0
```

You could check your work with ifconfig(8), but that's boring. Ping your floating IP and you should get an answer. Then look at `ifconfig`.

```
# ifconfig carp89
carp89: flags=8843<UP,BROADCAST,RUNNING,SIMPLEX,MULTICAST> mtu 1500
    lladdr 00:00:5e:00:01:58
    index 6 priority 15 llprio 3
    carp: MASTER carpdev em0 vhid 89 advbase 1 advskew 100
    groups: carp
    status: master
    inet 192.0.2.100 netmask 0xffffff00 broadcast 192.0.2.255
```

While this looks much like any other interface, take a look at the lladdr line. This MAC ends in 58, which is hexadecimal for the VHID. The CARP master always uses the same MAC address, so that the IP address becomes available as soon as the network switch notices the port change.

The CARP line gives the CARP-specific information we set. This host was configured as the preferred backup—so why is it the master? It's the master because it's the only host in this redundancy group. When another host claims the master role, this host should gracefully surrender the master role.

Once you test the new floating IP and verify that it works, create an */etc/hostname.carp89* file so that OpenBSD configures this interface at boot. It should contain everything that was in your ifconfig command except the interface you're configuring.

```
vhid 89 pass PetRats carpdev em0 advskew 100 \
    192.0.2.100 netmask 255.255.255.0
```

Now configure the master.

Configuring Non-Backup Hosts

Configure hosts that aren't the assigned backup almost exactly the same, but don't set an advskew value. If a host is the master, or if you don't care which host is regularly the master, configure them both like so.

```
# ifconfig interface vhid vhidnumber pass password \
    carpdev interface ip netmask mask
```

Our actual command line on the new master server looks much like the backup server. I'm too lazy to type that netmask again, though, so we'll use modern slash notation instead.

```
# ifconfig carp89 vhid 89 pass PetRats carpdev \
  em0 192.0.2.100/24
```

A ping-based test won't tell if this CARP interface is correct or not. Take a look at `ifconfig`.

If you enabled preemption on both hosts, your preferred master should have automatically become the master.

If it worked as expected, create an `/etc/hostname.carp89` file with the interface configuration.

```
vhid 89 pass PetRats carpdev em0 192.0.2.100/24
```

When your master host fails, the backup will become master. But let's test that.

Failover Testing

Untested failover isn't failover. It's hope. And a weak hope, at that. Always test failover before going live. Test it again during every maintenance window.

On an unrelated host, set up a continuous ping of the floating address. Then tell the current master to surrender the floating IP by setting the CARP interface to down.

```
# ifconfig carp89 down
```

The ex-master launches a flood of announcements declaring "I'm going down! Abandon ship! Someone, quick, save the floating IP!" The backup immediately declares itself the master. Your client shouldn't drop a ping.

You can see failovers in real time by watching `/var/log/messages`. I often use `tail -f` on the log files of both hosts while testing failover.

To have the manually failed host rejoin the redundancy group, turn the interface back up. You can combine shutdown and reactivation in a single command, so that if no other CARP host is available this host will pick the address right back up.

```
# ifconfig carp89 down && ifconfig carp89 up
```

Once you can manually fail the cluster back and forth, try some less graceful failover. Simulate a power or network failure—probably by pulling a cord, although you can use an axe if you wish. The backup should notice and become master in a second or less. Bounce the master back and forth a few times to verify failover works as you expect.

Once you're satisfied that CARP-based failover works, configure a web site.

CARP and Httpd

Network-facing programs normally can only bind to IP addresses on the system. CARP requires thinking about that a little more. When a host is a CARP backup, the floating IP is weakly attached to the system. It's not active, but it's there. Programs can bind to it, but nobody can actually reach that server on that host. If the CARP backup tries to connect to the floating IP it traverses the network to the master, even though it has that same IP weakly bound to itself.

This means you can use the floating IP in program configurations like *httpd.conf*. A host's web server will only be reachable from the network when it's the master.

Should you configure a web server so that it's unreachable unless it's in use? That depends entirely on your organization. I might have the server listen only on the floating IP, or I might have it listening on multiple IPs so I can monitor the port while the server is in the backup state.

Configure a simple web site that shows nothing but the server name on each of your CARP servers. Fail back and forth a few times and check the site with your web browser. You'll probably have to force a reload as discussed in Chapter 0, because servers and clients alike don't like unnecessary traffic.

This works well until the web site goes down, of course. If the httpd process dies, we need the host to step out of the master role and let the other take over.

CARP Demotion

CARP includes a *demotion counter* on each interface. The host with the lowest demotion counter is chosen to be master. A host can use the demotion counter to communicate with PF and say "Hey wait, I'm not ready yet!" or "Okay, now you can go."

OpenBSD includes ifstated(8), a program to check the state of interfaces and programs. You can use this program to check if httpd(8) is running, and feed demotion and undemotion notices to the host's CARP interfaces.

You'll need an */etc/ifstated.conf* that checks to see if httpd is running. This example checks every 10 seconds. If httpd is running and has been running, it leaves everything alone. If httpd stopped running since the last check, it demotes the CARP interfaces. If httpd has started running after being stopped, the CARP interface is undemoted.

```
daemon_up = '( "rcctl httpd check" every 10 )'

state main {
  if !$daemon_up {
    run "ifconfig -g carp carpdemote"
    set-state demoted
  }
}

state demoted {
  if $daemon_up {
    run "ifconfig -g carp -carpdemote"
    set-state main
  }
}
```

Now enable ifstated in */etc/rc.conf.local*.

```
ifstated_flags=""
```

Congratulations! You now have a web server cluster. For load balancing that can actually do some balancing, you need relayd.

Chapter 9: Your Relayd Host

A load balancer is a packet filtering firewall with extra mojo. A packet filtering firewall is a nosy router. Before you can configure load balancing, you need a functional packet filter setup. This chapter discusses installing and configuring a host for a standalone load balancer. While this chapter assumes you're using relayd to distribute load to a group of web servers, it applies whether you're building a standard reverse proxy, an SSL accelerator (Chapter 14), or a proxy (Chapter 15). It also applies if you're distributing traffic to hosts other than web servers. We'll build on this material in Chapter 16 to build a relayd cluster.

A relayd host separates your web server hosts from a larger network—perhaps the global Internet, or perhaps just your organization. I'll call this larger network "the world," but it could be any entity needed. Your relayd box should have at least two network interfaces, including VLANs. Connect these interfaces to different network segments. Put your web server hosts on one segment and connect the other to the outside world. Putting all of these on the same network segment is possible, but it's terrible practice and will cause you great pain.[20]

Relayd distributes traffic via NAT. You can use private addresses for the web servers. You might or might not want your server subnet routed to the relayd host, depending on your security stance, network topology, and biases.

---

20   If you dare to complain about that pain, people will laugh at you.

113

Once you have the machine installed and the latest OpenBSD release installed, proceed to configuring the host.

Setup Considerations

We'll take an incremental approach to installing the relayd host. The installation process is broken up into groups of tasks. Verify each group is not only complete, but functional and survives a reboot before proceeding. I've spent hours debugging packet filters only to discover that the host isn't forwarding packets. Don't be like me.

The aggressive configuration used here is designed to protect both your network and others. While you can't ensure that nobody can break into that awful web application you need to run, you can prevent the intruder from spawning a reverse shell from your web server. It's not a fix for the application, but it reduces the damage your intruder can inflict.

For these examples, I assume that you are managing the host through the same interface and IP address you're using to provide service. When I design an enterprise network, I put in a series of management VLANs for other management activities. This lets me separate traffic from the host's role, such as web serving, from administrative traffic like SSH. Each host has a separate physical interface for each. This is a great way to do things… if you have the luxury of designing your environment from scratch.

Whatever you do, don't do a partial setup and deploy with the intent of "fixing it later." You mean to come back to the task, I'm sure. You really, sincerely mean to. But if there's no time to do it correctly at deployment, there's no time to fix it later.

Network Configuration

A relayd box starts life as a packet filter, but a packet filter starts its life as a router. During the initial router setup, you'll find checking your work easiest if at least one host outside the relayd box routes the private subnet to the relayd host.

For our example setup, the outside world segment uses the IP address range 203.0.113.0/24. The web servers to be balanced use the private subnet of 192.0.2.0/24. Our relayd host has one interface in each subnet, em0 at 203.0.113.213 and em1 at 192.0.2.1.

To make interfaces easier to differentiate and to make configuration simpler, add each interface to a group named after its function. The default route is on the em0 interface, so OpenBSD will automatically assign it to be part of the *egress* interface group. Here's `/etc/hostname.em0`.

```
inet 203.0.113.213/24
```

Interface em1 is connected to the server farm, so I create the *farm* group for it. The `/etc/hostname.em1` file will look like so.

```
inet 192.0.2.1/24
group farm
```

The host needs to be able to forward packets between interfaces. Set `net.inet.ip.forwarding` to 1 in `/etc/sysctl.conf`.

```
net.inet.ip.forwarding=1
```

Reboot.

Configure a web host on the private subnet to use the relayd host as a gateway. In this case, that means setting its default route to 192.0.2.1.

You need an external test host. If the private subnet isn't routed to the relayd box, pick a test host on the network segment immediately attached to the relayd host's external interface. Add a route for the private subnet to that test host, using the relayd machine's external IP as the gateway. If the private subnet is routed, you can test with any unfiltered host on your network.

Once the relayd host finishes rebooting, the web host should be able to ping and traceroute the relayd machine's private interface, the relayd machine's egress interface, and your external test host. The external test host should be able to ping and traceroute the relayd host's two interfaces and the web host.

If the server subnet is routed within your organization, the web host should be able to traceroute within your organization. If the server subnet uses public IP addresses, it should be able to traceroute globally.

If these don't work, you did something wrong. Solve any problems before proceeding.

Once you're convinced everything works, remove any temporary routes.

Packet Filtering

Now that the router can pass packets, stop most of the packets from passing. While most firewalls exist to give a trusted network Internet access without letting the Internet access most of the trusted network, relayd machines have a different role.

While I might trust OpenBSD as a web server, I don't trust whatever random application the organization wants to deploy on that server. If that application is breached, I need to protect both the relayd box and the public Internet from their mayhem.

My web servers can only initiate very limited traffic to the public Internet. I permit access to select DNS servers, a specific web site for OpenBSD updates, and traceroute. Choose an access level that fits your paranoia.

Macros

As is usual in any PF install, reused elements go in macros. You might put macros in an include file for easier updating.

My organization has a specific list of hosts permitted to perform system management. These might be static IPs assigned to sysadmin desktops, monitoring stations, or similar hosts. I define the *mgmt* macro for these hosts.

```
mgmt="{203.0.113.70, 198.51.100.0/24}"
```

We need PF macros for our web servers. I might move web servers around, and individual web servers might have their own rules—say, for SSH. The easiest way for me to cope with this is to have a separate macro for each server, then combine the macros into the list.

```
www1="192.0.2.100"
www2="192.0.2.101"
```

I define a couple of DNS servers the web servers can use. Here I piggyback off of Google.

```
dns="{8.8.8.8 8.8.4.4}"
```

I'll use these macros throughout the filter configuration.

Blocking Bogons

IP networks that should never appear on the network are called *bogons* or *martians*. RFC 5735 lists the standard bogon addresses. I'll list these in a separate file for easier updates, include the file in my rules, and drop these addresses.

My /etc/rfc5735.conf file looks much like this.

```
table <rfc5735> { 0.0.0.0/8 10.0.0.0/8 127.0.0.0/8 \
   169.254.0.0/16 172.16.0.0.12 192.0.0.0/24 \
   192.0.2.0/24 192.88.99.0/24 192.168.0.0/16 \
   198.18.0.0/15 198.51.100.0/24 203.0.113.0/24 \
   224.0.0.0/4 240.0.0.0/4 255.255.255.255/32 }
```

I'll remove any addresses that are actually used on my network.

Managing Web Servers

How are you going to manage your web hosts? There's no great way to multiplex several machines' worth of a host-specific service like SSH onto a single IP.

If you are the only sysadmin, you might SSH to the relayd box and then to the individual web hosts. That doesn't scale—separation of privilege requires that your web developers not have access to the load balancer.

The OpenBSD examples suggest using a CARP cluster behind the relayd box and forwarding all SSH traffic to that host. You'll need the same SSH host keys on all of the CARP hosts, but it works just fine.

As reading about things that exist in the examples is boring, I'm going to assign each web host an SSH port on the relayd box. Any traffic to that port gets redirected to port 22 on the specific web host. That simplifies system management through tools such as Ansible and Puppet.

Now that you know what we're doing, let's go through the rules.

/etc/pf.conf

Once I have the macros in place, I'll pull in the include file. I want to log on the egress interface, and return errors for refused connections.

```
include "/etc/rfc5735.conf"
set loginterface egress
set block-policy return
```

There's no reason to filter on the localhost interface. We also need to polish incoming and outgoing traffic. Finally, I add the anchor where relayd adds its rules. You must have this anchor to use relayd.

```
set skip on lo0
match in all scrub (no-df random-id max-mss 1440)
anchor "relayd/*"
```

Now add actual filter rules. The first line below configures NAT for all networks behind the relayd box, so that any traffic we choose to pass gets translated. The second and third lines reject all bogons. The fourth rule defines a global "deny all" rule. As PF works on a "last matching rule wins" basis, any traffic you want to pass must be explicitly defined. Finally, the fifth rule permits the relayd box itself to make any connections it wants.

```
match out on egress inet from !(egress:network) \
    to any nat-to (egress:0)
block in quick on egress from <rfc5735> to any
block in quick on egress from any to <rfc5735>
block all
pass out quick inet
```

Now let's let some traffic leave from the server farm. We permit DNS to our chosen name servers as well as HTTP to our chosen update server.

```
pass in on farm proto { tcp udp } from (farm:network) \
    to $dns port 53
pass in on farm proto tcp from (farm:network) to \
    ftp3.usa.openbsd.org port 80
```

Never block all ICMP. You can fine-tune ICMP to permit only the necessary components, but if an intruder has penetrated a web server so deeply that she can funnel information out via carefully crafted ICMP packets, you need better security monitoring. Allowing the UDP component of traceroute(8) is optional but highly useful.

```
pass in on farm proto icmp from (farm:network) \
    to (farm:0)
pass in proto udp to port 33433 >< 33626
pass in on egress proto icmp from any to (egress)
```

Now there's traffic from the outside world coming in. My management addresses can do anything. Each web server gets its own port redirection for SSH.

```
pass in on egress from $mgmt
pass in on egress proto tcp from $mgmt to \
  (egress:0) port 2201 rdr-to $www1 port 22
pass in on egress proto tcp from $mgmt to \
  (egress:0) port 2202 rdr-to $www2 port 22
```

Finally, the web server farm cannot communicate with the relayd server on any TCP port.

```
block in on farm proto {tcp, udp} from \
  (farm:network) to (farm:0)
```

Verify that your packet filter passes the traffic you expect and blocks everything else.

PF Maximum States and Relayd

While it's rare to have a web server max out PF's state table, it can certainly happen with a heavily-loaded load balancer. The default size of the state table is 10,000. To see the current number of state table entries, use pfctl(8).

```
# pfctl -ss | wc -l
```

Adjust the maximum limit with the `set limit states` option in `pf.conf`.

```
set limit states 20000
```

If your clients start getting "connection refused" messages, check your state table.

I've hit this limit often enough that I habitually monitor the size of the state table. Once I hit 75% of the maximum during peak hours, I increase the limit. Increasing a system's memory use, or even adding RAM, is infinitely less expensive than me having to explain to the boss why the load balancer broke.

Once you're sure the packet filter is running correctly, you're ready to deploy relayd.

Chapter 10: Relayd Essentials

Relayd inspects incoming network traffic and redirects it to other hosts. You can use relayd to balance traffic based on load, wrap applications in SSL, inspect application traffic, and more. Relayd can make decisions based on TCP/IP characteristics and application-level traffic. Many vendors sell commercial appliances to do these same things, calling them "application redirectors" or "reverse proxies" or just plain old "load balancers." I'll refer to a relayd installation as a load balancer, because that's the most common use, but it can serve all of these roles. Similarly, while relayd can distribute traffic for many applications, I usually refer to the servers as web servers.

The main parts of a load balancer are relayd(8) itself, the configuration file */etc/relayd.conf*, and the relayctl(8) management program.

relayd(8)

The relayd program has four main components: the parent process, a host check engine, a PF engine, and a relay engine.

The relayd parent process handles privileged tasks like network configuration, reading the configuration file, and running external programs. It sends the other components any information they need. The parent process runs as **root**, so the other processes don't have to.

The *host check engine* or *HCE* investigates potential relay targets. It makes sure a web server is up before sending traffic to that server. It has several built-in checking methods, or you can use an external script. When your flunky Bill accidentally runs newfs(8) a production server, the HCE notices and informs the PF engine.

The *PF engine* creates and removes PF redirection rules in PF anchors. It also updates PF tables.

The *relay engine* listens to the network. It performs any higher-level protocol inspection you've set up, then hands connections off to the final destination.

Relayd takes most of its instructions from the configuration file. To check if the configuration is valid, run `relayd -n`. Remember, a "valid" configuration is not the same as "a configuration that does what I want."

Specify an alternate configuration file with `-f`. It's common to create a test configuration in a separate file, verify that it's valid, and then copy it into place.

```
# relayd -nf /etc/relayd.conf.test
configuration OK
```

To make relayd more verbose, add `-v`.

When you're testing or debugging relayd, you might want to run it in foreground mode. This keeps `relayd` from daemonizing and puts all the output to the terminal. This quickly becomes overwhelming on an active system, however. The relayctl(8) program includes features to watch relayd as it performs tests and makes changes. We'll use relayctl(8) throughout the last half of this book.

You could also redefine macros on the command line, which might be useful for testing. Use `-D` and the new macro setting.

```
# relayd -dv -D www1="192.0.2.111"
```

Where do these macros come from? The relayd configuration file `/etc/relayd.conf`, of course.

/etc/relayd.conf

The file `/etc/relayd.conf` contains all relayd configuration. The file looks an awful lot like `httpd.conf` and other OpenBSD configurations.

Each group of servers you want to load balance needs its own table, much like a PF table. You can then use that table to define a rule. Here's a complete, working `relayd.conf` for a small farm of two web servers.

```
table <www> {192.0.2.101 192.0.2.102}
redirect www {
    listen on 203.0.113.213 port 80 interface em0
    forward to <www> check http "/" code 200
}
```

Let's take this apart.

The first line defines a table called *www*. Relayd tables deliberately resemble PF tables, but the two programs don't share tables. This table contains two IP addresses. Presumably, this table is for web services and the addresses are your web servers. Don't use misleading names for your tables unless you want your coworkers to have a new reason to hate you.

The next line opens a *redirect*, which a simple TCP forwarder using PF redirection rules. The curly braces contain all configuration for this redirect.

The third line defines where this redirect opens a network socket. This *listen* statement attaches this redirect to IP address 203.0.113.213 on interface em0.

The *forward* statement on the fourth line provides instructions for the PF engine and the host check engine. This line is the real brains of the relayd configuration. Incoming connections are forwarded to hosts in the www table defined at the top of the file. The check statement gives instructions to the host check engine, though. The HCE does an HTTP GET on each server. If it receives a code 200 response (also known as an OK), relayd can choose to send traffic to that server. If it gets any other code or no response, that server is removed from the pool.

Macros

The `relayd.conf` file supports macros, just like those in PF and `httpd.conf`. Macros let you reuse configuration information throughout a file. Put macros at the top of the file. You'll most commonly use macros for server addresses, so changes can easily propagate through your configuration. I've never regretted using macros. I have occasionally regretted not using macros. Use macros.

While our sample configuration seems small enough to not need macros, here's what it would look like with them.

```
www1="192.0.2.101"
www2="192.0.2.102"
ext_ip="203.0.113.213"

table <www> {$www1 $www2}
redirect www {
   listen on $ext_ip port 80 interface em0
   forward to <www> check http "/" code 200
}
```

As your configuration expands—and it will—you'll find macros increasingly useful.

Global Configuration

Any global configuration options go at the top of `relayd.conf`. This includes logging parameters, the number of processes to start, timeouts, and more. We'll cover global options throughout the rest of the book.

Our sample configuration has no global options, because the defaults work pretty well.

Tables

Tables contain lists of servers relayd can direct traffic to. They go after macros and the global configuration options, but before any relaying rules.

Hosts within tables can be separated by spaces, commas, or new-lines. Tables can also have additional attributes, as discussed in Chapter 11.

Includes

You can use an include statement to pull other files into `relayd.conf`. You might have separate relayd configurations for multiple services, or perhaps a server-wide macro file.

```
include "/etc/macros.conf"
```

Include files can be a great way to manage complicated configurations, or a complete nightmare. Use what works for you.

Redirections, Relays, and More

The beginning of the configuration files builds a foundation for the traffic distribution rules. Later chapters discuss redirections, relays, protocols, and routers.

To see what relayd is doing, you need relayctl(8).

relayctl(8)

The relayctl(8) program gives visibility into the current state of relayd. It communicates with a running relayd instance through a socket. The relayctl program is complicated only because relayd supports so many types of load balancing. When we cover a type of load balancing we'll look at the corresponding relayctl(8) subcommands.

The simplest relayctl command is to tell relayd to spill its current configuration with the `show summary` subcommand. This lists all of the configured hosts, tables, and redirections, relays, and everything else you've set up. Here's the summary for our simple relayd setup.

```
# relayctl show summary
Id  Type       Name           Avlblty  Status
1   redirect   www                     active
1   table      www:80                  active (2 hosts)
1   host       192.0.2.101    100.00%  up
2   host       192.0.2.102    100.00%  up
```

All relayctl output shares these five headings. The first column, *id*, assigns each type of item a unique number. Yes, the number 1 appears multiple times in the output above—but there's only one redirect 1, one table 1, and one host 1. The type shows what relayd feature we're looking at, such as a redirect or a host. You configured the name in `relayd.conf`. Availability gives a percent uptime to each host. Items such as tables and relays and redirects don't have an availability. Finally, the status tells us if the item is functional or not.

The first line tells us that we configured a redirection called www, and that it's running. The next three lines discuss the host table for that redirection.

You can abbreviate each word in a relayctl(8) subcommand, so long as you leave enough to uniquely identify the subcommand. If you're familiar with Cisco routers and switches, this will look familiar.

```
# relayctl sh su
```

Let's look at hosts next.

Viewing Hosts

Are your web servers working? More importantly, does relayd think that your web servers are working? To see what relayd thinks of all the hosts in your server farm, use the `show hosts` subcommand.

```
# relayctl sh hosts
Id  Type     Name               Avlblty Status
1   table    www:80                     active (2 hosts)
1   host     192.0.2.101        29.73%  up
             total: 22/74 checks
2   host     192.0.2.102        55.41%  up
             total: 41/74 checks
```

The first line beneath the header gives the name of our host table, *www*. The status shows as active, with two hosts, so it's working.

Below that is an entry for the first host in this table, 192.0.2.101. It's availability is 29.73%, but it's currently up. The line beneath shows that it's passed 22 out of 74 HCE tests. This is not a healthy host.

Last is an entry for the host 192.0.2.102. It's slightly more reliable than the previous host, having passed 41 out of 74 HCE tests.

Each host and table also has a unique ID number, shown in the first column. It's slightly confusing because tables are shown intermingled with hosts. Table 1 is "www." Host 1 is 192.0.2.101, while host 2 is 192.0.2.102. Some configuration options require this number.

Disabling, Enabling, and Checking Hosts

Eventually you'll want to do maintenance on your hosts. While you could simply yank a web server's power cord and let relayd figure out that the host is down, you might want to proactively tell relayd to remove that host from the pool and stop the HCE from checking it. Use the `host disable` subcommand and the host's IP address.

```
# relayctl host disable 192.0.2.101
command succeeded
```

If you do a `relayctl show hosts`, this host's status appears as `disabled`.

Use the `host enable` subcommand to put that host back in the pool. The HCE starts poking at the host, and adds it back to the pool if it passes.

To tell the HCE to immediately check all hosts, use the `poll` subcommand.

```
# relayctl poll
command succeeded
```

Chapter 11 discusses configuring checks, including check timing.

Configuration Management

You can use OpenBSD's rcctl(8) to tell relayd to read its configuration file, but you can also use relayctl(8). The reload subcommand tells relayd to reread the configuration file it was started with, probably */etc/relayd.conf*.

```
# relayctl reload
```

If you want a running relayd to read in a new configuration file and use it, use the load subcommand and the file. This lets you swap out configurations without restarting.

```
# relayctl load /etc/relayd.conf.maintenance
```

This feature isn't available through rcctl(8).

Watching and Logging Relayd

Relayd provides a few different ways to watch it: through relayctl(8), through the log, and even via SNMP.

Live Monitoring

Use the `relayctl monitor` command to receive real-time status messages from a running relayd process. These messages are internal to relayd and not really designed to be easily understood, but you can glean a fair amount from them.

If you have an SNMP infrastructure, you can send an SNMP trap whenever relayd notices that the state of a host changes. SNMP traps are global commands in *relayd.conf*. By default relayd sends the trap to a socket at */var/run/agentx.sock*, the default for OpenBSD's snmpd(8), but you can specify an alternate path as an argument.

```
snmp trap "/var/run/net-snmp.sock"
```

For less realtime monitoring, use logs.

Relayd Logging

Logs are good. You need logs. But what kind of logs do you need? Most of relayd does very little logging, but the host check engine can perform additional logging. Relayd has three logging levels: default, brief, and verbose.

By default, relayd doesn't log much beyond "hi, I've started" and "goodbye, I'm leaving." The *brief* log level records when a host changes state. At the *verbose* level, the HCE logs every time it examines a host. Enable and disable such logging with `relayd.conf` statements and relayctl(8).

Tell the HCE to use brief logs with the `relayd.conf` option `log updates`. If you want to log every time the HCE pokes at a host, use `log all`.

`log updates`

You can use relayctl(8) to tell relayd to change the current logging level with the *log* subcommand. Using the `log verbose` subcommand tells relayd to log all host checks, while `log brief` tells it to log only host updates.

```
# relayctl log verbose
logging request sent.
```

You can't use relayctl to return the logging level to the nearly empty default, however.

The verbose log goes to syslogd with a facility of daemon and a priority of debug. OpenBSD doesn't record these messages by default. You could add an entry to record debugging output from every daemon, but that gets ugly quick. Instead, add an entry to `/etc/syslog.conf` to pull relayd messages into their own log file.

```
!relayd
*.*  /var/log/relayd
```

Syslogd(8) won't create files, so you must make the file before re-starting syslogd.

```
# touch /var/log/relayd
# rcctl restart syslogd
```

Now that you can keep an eye on relayd, let's consider how it makes decisions.

Chapter 11: The Host Check Engine and Traffic Modes

The Host Check Engine or HCE is the heart of how relayd guides traffic. It determines which hosts can receive traffic and which can't. While the HCE's default settings are suitable for a variety of environments, large or complex setups will need tweaking. And once you have the HCE validating host availability just the way you want it to, you can adjust how relayd distributes traffic between those hosts.

The most obvious place to tune the HCE is in its timing.

Host Check Timing, Scheduling, and Retries

The HCE doesn't constantly check host availability; rather, it checks at ten second intervals. If the host responds to the request within two hundred milliseconds, the host is considered available. Depending on your application, your uptime needs, and your monitoring requirements, you might need to adjust these times or change how it treats failures.

Check Interval

Adjust the amount of time between HCE checks with the *interval* option. You can set this as a global option or on a per-check basis. If you're only load balancing a single service, a global option is fine.

```
interval 5
```

If you have multiple services and need to tune the interval for one of them, you'll want to set the interval in a forward statement.

```
forward to <www> check http "/" code 200 interval 20
```

Intervals set in the forward statement must be multiples of the default interval. If you have one service that needs an interval of 3 seconds and several hundred that need the default, you'll need to set the global interval to 3 and override all the others to use either 9 or 12 seconds.

Check Timeout

The *timeout* option controls the number of milliseconds the HCE will wait for a response before marking the host down. Every check but ICMP uses the timeout value. (ICMP checks can only use the global timeout setting.) Much like setting the interval, timeout can be set globally or per-check. A per-check timeout does not need to be a multiple of the global timeout.

```
timeout 100
…
    forward to <www> check http "/" code 200 timeout 45
…
```

The more stuff you have between the relayd box and the server hosts, the more likely you'll need to increase the timeout. If everything's on the same subnet on the same switch, the default is not only fine but it might be high. Put a router in the middle and you might need to increase it to a second or so. Cross-country checks require higher times, and also indicate you should seriously reevaluate your entire architecture.

Retries

The HCE is strict. If a host fails, it fails. It gets no second chances. If you want the HCE to check a host multiple times before flagging it as down and removing it from the active server list, use the *retry* option. For most environments, adjusting retries increases the amount of downtime users experience.

Set this option for each host in a table separately.

```
table <www> { $www1 $www2 retry 2 }
```

The host represented by $www2 gets retried twice, for a total of three checks, before being marked down. Using the default relayd interval of ten seconds, this host must be down for 30 seconds or longer before relayd stops sending traffic to it.

The host represented by $www1 has no retry value, however. If it fails a host check, it is immediately marked as down and removed from service.

When a table needs per-host values, listing each host on its own line makes more sense.

```
table <www> {
   $www1 retry 2
   $www2 retry 2 }
```

This arrangement highlights configuration inconsistencies.

Tweaking Host Tests

If you're using hosts with multiple addresses, or load balancing for hosts on another network, you might want to adjust how the HCE performs its tests.

Multiple Address Web Servers

If your host has multiple IP addresses, and you want to include more than one of those addresses in a table, that's fine. The catch is, the HCE will check each of those addresses for availability. Most often you won't want to check a single host multiple times. You can use the `relayd.conf` parent directive to tell relayd that a table entry is attached to another host, and should not be checked separately.

Identify a parent by host number. Get the host number from `relayctl show hosts.` as discussed in Chapter 10. That example shows that the host 192.0.2.101 is host 1, while 192.0.2.102 is host 2. Here I've set up another table, where one of the new hosts is located on the second of those.

```
table <www> { 192.0.2.101 192.0.2.102 }
table <app> { 192.0.1.202 parent 2 192.0.2.203 }
```

Relayd will not perform health checks on the host 192.0.1.202; it will use the health checks of 192.0.2.102 to measure that host's availability.

If you have multiple servers with parents, each needs its own parent statement. As with the retry statement, you might find giving each server its own line in the configuration easier to manage.

Remote Servers

Load balancing gets even more complicated when you're using web servers on remote networks. The Internet is a tangled, complicated mess of interconnections and routes. Any network engineer can share delightful tales of how sites that were two hops away yesterday suddenly became thirty hops away, or how traffic to the office on the other side of town suddenly got routed through a country on the other side of the world thanks to some new tech on another continent misconfiguring their router.

You probably decided to redirect traffic to remote servers because they weren't terribly remote. The Internet's complexity can destroy that assumption, though. A server might respond to a host check quickly enough, but be so distant that performance with an actual application is dreadful. You can ensure that potential servers in the pool are close enough by adjusting the IP packet's time-to-live with the *ip ttl* option in `relayd.conf`. Each host in a table needs its own ip ttl statement.

```
table <www> {
   $www1 ip ttl 3
   $www2 ip ttl 3}
```

The packets for the host checks will have their time-to-live set to three. Each router in the path decrements the TTL by one. If the vagaries of the Internet mean that the host somehow becomes more than three hops away, the checks cannot reach the host. The host check will fail.

The TTL feature was added to relayd specifically for the router feature. If you want to load balance multiple Internet connections without going into BGP, OSPF, or proprietary solutions, definitely check out relayd's router function.

Host Check Methods

Checking to see if the web server can return a 200 code is a decent way to test generic web server functionality. A complicated application needs more sophisticated checking, however. Here we'll go through relayd's host checking methods.

Define all host check methods in a forward statement. Not all host check types can be used on all types of host. While the examples here mostly use redirects, that's only because redirects are the only type of relayd configuration we've seen yet. Host checks work just as well on relays (Chapter 13) and other traffic management methods.

Ping Test

Maybe you don't care if the web server is running or not; you only want to know if the host exists. The ICMP check pings each host in the pool. If the host answers the ping, it's in.

```
redirect www {
    listen on $ext_ip port 80 interface em0
    forward to <fallback> check icmp
}
```

An ICMP test is sensible for certain routing configurations, or for servers where there is no fallback. If your "Our site is undergoing maintenance" server is down with everything else, you're pretty much sunk.

TCP Port Test

Slightly more sophisticated is checking to see if a TCP port is open and accepting traffic. A TCP host check doesn't exchange any application data with the server, but only tests to see if a port is open. This is most useful for applications without more advanced tests. Here's a simple check to see if anything's running on port 25 on your hosts.

```
redirect smtp {
    listen on $ext_ip port 25 interface em0
    forward to <smtp> check tcp
}
```

Theoretically, port 25 means a mail server. This kind of check assumes that if the port is accepting connections the daemon running on the port is accepting traffic. This is not a reliable test—the kernel accepts the connection, then passes it off to the daemon. If you know anything about the protocol, or if you can write an external check script for the service, you can verify what's running on the server, as discussed later this chapter.

The TCP check inherits the port from the listen statement above it. If this particular redirection is listening on port 25, it checks port 25. You can change this behavior with a port keyword in the check statement.

```
redirect smtp {
    listen on $ext_ip port 25 interface em0
    forward to <smtp> check tcp port 65025
}
```

This lets you run software that doesn't use privilege separation on high-numbered ports, so it doesn't require **root** for network access.

(That software might need **root** privileges for other reasons, but not to bind to a low-numbered port.)

TLS Check

The TLS check determines if the service listening on a port can support a complete TLS conversation. It doesn't verify certificate validity, merely that whatever's attached to the port can speak TLS. This is slightly more reliable than checking the TCP port. While the kernel still accepts the connection, the daemon is what processes the TLS request.

```
redirect smtps {
   listen on $ext_ip port 587 interface em0
   forward to <www> check tls
}
```

As with TCP checks, the TLS checks inherit port numbers from the preceding listen statement. You can change the port as needed in the check itself.

```
redirect smtps {
   listen on $ext_ip port 587 interface em0
   forward to <www> check tls port 443
}
```

Only redirect traffic this way if someone else runs your web servers and you're trying to make them loathe you even more.

For average web applications, though, use one of relayd's built-in HTTP checks.

Check HTTP Response Code

Perhaps the most common type of host check is requesting a URL and checking the HTTP response code. Relayd calls this the *http check*. Chapter 10 included exactly such a check.

```
redirect www {
   listen on $ext_ip port 80 interface em0
   forward to <www> check http "/" code 200
}
```

137

The forward statement tells us which hosts to forward connections to, those in the table *www*. The check requests the path in the quote marks—in this case, a slash, for the site's main page. If the site returns the specified code, 200 in this case, the check succeeds. If it returns any other code, the check fails.

Some servers run multiple web sites. If you need to, you can specify the site's host name after the path with the `host` option.

```
forward to <www> check http "/" \
  host www.mallard.info code 200
```

Checking HTTP response codes can cause all sorts of frustration.[21] Theoretically a working page should return code 200, but the real world is messy and complicated and some web apps only add to the confusion. Before deploying a check based on HTTP response codes, test for yourself to see what response codes each host returns for your query. This is easy with printf(1) and nc(1).

```
$ printf "GET path HTTP/1.0\r\n\r\n" | \
  nc server port | head -n1
```

Suppose I want to check for the path /, on the host 192.0.2.102, on port 80. I'd run:

```
$ printf "GET / HTTP/1.0\r\n\r\n" | \
  nc www2.mallard.info 80 | head -n1
HTTP/1.0 200 OK
```

This server returns a 200 for this query. I could configure the load balancer with confidence. But a 301 or 302 wouldn't surprise me and would be nearly invisible to users.

If you must query for a particular site name, add that to the request like so.

---

21   I don't know how many times I've shrieked "But it works in my web browser!" while configuring load balancers. If you really want to know, though, my coworkers could probably tell you. They had a weekly pool.

```
$ printf "GET path HTTP/1.0\r\nHost: site\r\n\r\n" | \
  nc server port | head -n1
```

To query the same host for the site named www.mallard.info, we'd use this command.

```
$ printf "GET / HTTP/1.0\r\nHost: www.mallard.info\r\n\r\n" \
  | nc www2.mallard.info 80 | head -n1
HTTP/1.0 200 OK
```

Yes, it's a bit much to type, but it's much faster than trying to debug relayd by pounding your head on your laptop.

Check HTTP Response Code over TLS

Another common check is to look for a response code over TLS. Relayd calls this the https check. It'll look very similar to the http check, but works on port 443.

```
redirect https {
   listen on $ext_ip port 443 interface em0
   forward to <www> check https "/" code 200
}
```

If you have several TLS servers on the host, include a host name in the check so that relayd will query for that particular site.

```
redirect https {
   listen on $ext_ip port 443 interface em0
   forward to <www> check https "/" \
     host www4.mallard.info code 200
}
```

Just as with non-TLS sites, you'll want to validate that the web site returns the HTTP response code you expect. Telling relayd to expect a 200 when the server returns a 301, 302, or 404 will drive you to madness. Fortunately, OpenBSD's netcat nc(1) supports TLS, so we don't have to struggle with OpenSSL commands.

```
$ printf "GET / HTTP/1.0\r\nHost: site\r\n\r\n" | \
  nc -ce site host 443
```

Here I check the host 192.0.2.101 to see if the site www.mallard. info is available there over TLS.

```
$ printf "GET / HTTP/1.0\r\nHost: www.mallard.info\r\n\r\n" \
  | nc -ce www.mallard.info 192.0.2.101 443
```

If you paid attention in Chapter 6 and have OCSP stapling configured, you can add the `-T muststaple` option to nc(1) and validate the OCSP while you're at it. And while each web server should be identical, if you have trouble check each separately.

Check File Integrity

Relayd can also grab a text file from the web server and compute its SHA1 hash. You can use this in a couple different ways. Maybe you need to know that the web server is still delivering the correct files. I've also had complicated web apps perform a self-diagnostic every minute, running database queries and creating a status file that contains either the text "ok" or a diagnostic message. By checking the file hash, relayd can determine if the server should remain in service or not. We'll use this as our example, checking the digest of the file `/status`.

Remember that any change whatsoever in the file contents will change the hash value. You can't put dynamic content such as a timestamp in the hash file. Also, relayd expects the file contents to be a string. Don't point the digest check at a binary file like an image.

Before deploying file integrity tests, decide if you want clients to be able to access the status file. Will it hurt if a nosy user finds that http://www.mallard.info/status contains the word "ok?" Probably not, but the presence of the file will raise questions. It might even cause meetings. I usually put the status file on httpd's default server, which is a different virtual server than my main site. That way remote requests by IP address can get the status file, while clients browsing the site you really want to support can never see the status file.

First you'll need a status file. In the real world you'll start off with a fully tested, flexible, fault-tolerant monitoring script to regularly recreate it. For testing, though, you'll want a file that's known to be good.

Don't muck with the web hosts while you're trying to figure out load balancing. Create a status file on each of the hosts in the web farm.

```
# cd /var/www/htdocs
# echo ok > status
```

Verify that the load balancer can fetch the file from every host in the pool. Here I grab the status file from the host www1, at 192.0.2.101, and feed it to the next command. I'm not interested in the file itself, only the hash of the file, so I run it through sha(1)

```
$ ftp -o - http://192.0.2.101/status | sha1
Trying 192.0.2.101...
Requesting http://192.0.2.101/status
3 bytes received in 0.00 seconds (1.46 KB/s)
92a949fd41844e1bb8c6812cdea102708fde23a4
```

The long string at the end is the file's SHA1 hash. Use this in a http check in *relayd.conf*, but with the *digest* argument and the hash value.

```
redirect www {
    listen on $ext_ip port 80 interface em0
    forward to <www> check http "/status" digest 92a…
}
```

As long as the file */status* on each server in the pool has that same hash, the server remains in the pool. If relayd cannot retrieve the file, or if the hash of the file changes, the host is removed from the pool.

If your file is not on the default web site, set a hostname in the check statement.

```
…
forward to <www> check http "/status" \
    host www.mallard.info digest 92a...
…
```

You can perform the same check over TLS, using the https version of the check statement.

```
redirect https {
    listen on $ext_ip port 443 interface em0
    forward to <www> check https "/" \
        host www.mallard.info digest 92a…
}
```

Now all you need is that perfectly functioning health checking script on your application server. But that's a problem for the app developers, so you're done.[22]

Checking Hosts by Exchanging Data

Relayd's built-in HTTP checks are not complicated; they send a string and look for a code in the response. You can build many arbitrary services of your own using relayd's send/expect syntax, provided the protocol begins connections using plain text. Purely binary protocols require more sophisticated checking, but many daemons that use binary protocols (like SSH) offer a text-based banner at first connection.

Start by using nc(1) to learn how the service you want to watch opens a connection. Give two arguments, the host and the port. Here I check a mail server's port 25.

```
# nc mail.mallard.info 25
220 mail.mallard.info ESMTP Sendmail 8.15.2/8.15.2; Tue,
7 Feb 2017 15:52:32 -0500 (EST)
```

Connecting to the TCP port means that the kernel is accepting network connections. A response from the daemon attached to the port means that the daemon is actually functioning.

So what do we need to verify? The short answer is, enough to verify that mail is running, but not so much that the server fails the check for bogus reasons. The 220 code means that the mail server is ready to talk. The hostname should never change. Sendmail versions might

---

22   Unless you're both the app developer and the sysadmin, in which case you're pretty much doomed.

change, or (hopefully) be replaced outright, while the timestamp is certainly going to change. Checking for the 220 code should be enough to validate service, though.

Here's how we'd use a send/expect check in relayd.

```
redirect smtp {
    listen on $ext_ip port 25 interface em0
    forward to <smtp> check send "" expect "220 mail.mallard.info *"
}
```

We have to provide two pieces of information, the string to send and what we expect in return. The string we send is literal text, but for SMTP we don't have to send anything, so I use empty double quotes. Relayd will let you use the literal word *nothing* instead of two quotes.

The expected response can use shell globbing rules, just like we discussed in Chapter 3. The most commonly used glob here is an asterisk at the end, meaning "this string and a bunch of other stuff after." Here, relayd checks for the string `220 mail.mallard.info` and ignores everything after that text.

If the service uses TLS, add *tls* to the end of the check statement. This lets you check services like smtps.

The send/expect checks lets you determine if the host daemons are functioning. They might not be functioning *correctly*, mind you, but they're accepting connections and starting a conversation. More complicated function checks require scripting.

Host Check Scripts

Complicated applications can require complicated checks. With *check script*, relayd lets you call an external script to check host function. You might have a script that logs into each host's web site and verifies it returns the proper data, or a script that performs DNS lookups and verifies the nameserver is returning proper answers, or a script that actually sends mail through a mail server. These functionality checks can be as complex as needed.[23]

The server runs the script every time it needs to perform the host check, giving the server IP as an argument. If the check fails, the script must return 0. If the check is successful, the script can return any positive value. Yes, this is the opposite of what you might expect, but allows more scripting flexibility. Relayd runs the script as **_relayd**. At the end of the timeout value, relayd terminates the script. If you have a complicated script that checks many functions, you might need to increase the timeout.

The check script takes one argument, the full path to the script, in quotes.

```
relay dns dns {
    listen on $ext_ip port 53 interface em0
    forward to <dns> check script "/usr/local/scripts/dnscheck.sh"
}
```

If you have trouble with check scripts, separate the relayd configuration from the check script. The command /usr/bin/false always returns 1, so using it as your check script means that the host will always be up. Using /usr/bin/true as the check script declares the host always down.

But configuring relayd is the easy part. The more difficult part is the script. Depending on what you want to do, though, the script doesn't have to be that difficult. Write your check script as simply as possible, using the lightest language you can. Don't use Java when Perl will do, and don't use Perl when shell will do.

---

23   The *real* trick is to make scripts no more complex than needed.

Authoritative DNS Check

I have a group of DNS servers that should be authoritative for the domain mallard.info. I want to load balance them with relayd. If one of the servers stops returning authoritative answers, I want to remove it from the pool. Here I perform the DNS query using dig(1), and use grep(1) to test for an authoritative answer.

```
#!/bin/sh
```

```
! dig www.mallard.info @$1 | grep "qr aa rd" > /dev/null
```

The `dig` command notoriously returns a whole bunch of output. I don't care about the overwhelming majority of it. The *aa* flag indicates that this is an authoritative answer, and responses from my servers should always contain the *qr* and *rd* flags as well, so I have a nice consistent string I can check with grep(1). And I don't care about the output, so I throw it away.

The grep(1) command will return 1 if it finds a match, and 0 if there is no match. That's the exact opposite of what I want, so I stick an exclamation point in front of the whole command.

A shell script returns the return code of the last command that was run, so: we're done.

Put relayd in front of your authoritative nameserver cluster, and you can perform maintenance during normal business hours. Which is what all sysadmins want.

Modes

Once you know which hosts are functional, you'll need to distribute traffic between them. Relayd supports several different traffic distribution *modes*. Some load balancers call the mode the *scheduling algorithm*. Some of these modes are limited to either redirects or relays.

A few modes use hashes to distribute traffic. You can assign a permanent key for the hash in `relayd.conf`. Hashes must start with 0x and be 32 hexadecimal characters long. If you don't assign a hash, relayd generates a hash for you.

Assign the mode in the forward rule. Here I use TCP checks to shorten my examples, but you'll almost certainly want a more sophisticated check in production.

Relay and Redirect Modes

Certain modes can be used with both relays and redirects.

Relayd's default mode is *roundrobin*. Incoming connections are forwarded to active hosts on a rotating basis: first host 1, then host 2, then host 3, and so on. When you run out of hosts, relayd starts over again at host 1. This kind of load balancing is per connection, not per client. If a web farm has only one client, that client will get redirected to one server after another. If you don't specify a mode, you get roundrobin. Roundrobin mode actually occurs inside PF, rather than in relayd, as we'll see in Chapter 12.

```
forward to <www> check tcp mode roundrobin
```

Random mode scatters new connections randomly through your hosts. In random mode the number of connections to each host tends to even out, especially with large numbers of connections, but this isn't guaranteed. It's random.

```
forward to <www> check tcp mode random
```

The *source-hash* mode balances connections using the hash of the client's source address. Combined with a fixed hash in `relayd.conf`, source-hash makes traffic more consistent. Connections from a given IP will always get forwarded to a specific host.

```
forward to <www> check tcp mode source-hash 0xdeadbeef…
```

146

While the consistency of source-hash seems good, distributing traffic consistently can create problems. Relayd directs all traffic from a single IP address to a particular server. If that single IP is a NAT or proxy server with thousands of users behind it, that particular target server might melt down under load.

Redirect-Only Modes

The only mode restricted to only redirects is *least-states*. Relayd forwards new connections to whichever host has the fewest existing states.

```
forward to <www> check tcp mode least-states
```

Combined with careful tuning of the PF state table, using least-states can even out traffic load on a long-running load balancer.

Relay-Only Modes

Relays dig deeper into incoming traffic. This gives them additional ways to distribute traffic. Both of these methods can accept hashes. As with source-hash mode, hashing can cause all sorts of new problems.

The *loadbalance* mode tells the relay to distribute traffic based on a hash of the client source address, the relay's IP address, and the relay's port. This can help distribute incoming traffic from one client IP to multiple relays, but on a single service it's still prone to overloading a single host. Most of the time you'll want to use hash mode instead of loadbalance.

The *hash* mode uses the same input as loadbalance mode, but the relay can also feed additional information into the hash by using a protocol filter. It's designed for client cookies, as used in many PHP applications, but you could abuse it in other ways. Such filters can remediate the issues associated with hashing.

Relay and Redirect Timeouts

Each relay and redirect mode creates some sort of state, either in the relayd engine or PF. These states tell the load balancer how to forward traffic. As long as the connection is active, the state entry remains. The *session timeout* setting dictates how long in seconds relayd retains entries for idle sessions. The default is 600, or ten minutes. You can set this as low as you want, but absurdly short session timeouts increase the odds of you discovering new edge cases in your application. You could increase this to any value up to 2,147,483,647 seconds, or roughly 68 years.

```
redirect www {
    listen on $ext_ip port 80
    forward to <www> check http "/" code 200
    session timeout 150
}
```

I would encourage you to leave the session timeout alone unless your application vendor or developer specifically recommends adjusting the load balancer idle timeout.

Remember that relayd rips out all PF table entries and loses all internal state when the process terminates, so absurdly long timeouts effectively mean "as long as this relayd process lasts."[24]

Now that you understand the various ways relayd can check hosts, let's dive deep into redirections.

---

24   While no process in history has run for 68 years, OpenBSD has already dealt with the 2038 issue, so it's at least conceivable.

Chapter 12: Redirections

Redirections are perhaps the simplest sort of relayd load balancing. A redirection adds a pf(4) rule to direct traffic to one of the web hosts. It performs no protocol inspection and doesn't alter the contents in any way. A redirection lets you distribute load between multiple servers based strictly on TCP/IP characteristics.[25]

While we used simple redirection rules as examples in the previous two chapters, let's take a deeper look into how these powerful tools work.

Configuring Redirections

A redirection requires a listen and a forward statement.

The *listen* statement tells relayd where to listen for traffic coming to the host. The listen statement needs an IP address and a port where external clients will look for the service. Relayd doesn't normally open a network socket on the local host; instead, incoming TCP/IP requests make the kernel poke relayd, which creates a PF rule for that connection.

The *forward* statement tells relayd what kind of PF rules to create and how to manage them. This is where you define the load balancing mode and the way to test hosts to see if they're ready to accept traffic.

Here's a complete `relayd.conf` that contains a single redirection. While using macros would be better practice, I've deliberately made this as small as possible.

---

25   If this confuses you, immediately grab a copy of the newest edition of Hansteen's The Book of PF. Once you have it, *read* it.

```
table <web> {192.0.2.101 192.0.2.102}

redirect www {
  listen on 203.0.113.213 port 80
  forward to <web> check http "/" code 200
}
```

The first line creates a table called "web" that lists our private web servers, 192.0.2.101 and 192.0.2.102. Immediately after that we define the redirection called "www."

Relayd listens for connections coming to the IP 203.0.113.213, on port 80. We could add an interface statement here as some earlier examples show, but it's not required. Outside hosts see this site as being at 203.0.113.213, just like any other NAT'd web server.

The forward rule tells relayd to create a PF rule that forwards traffic to the hosts in the www table. Relayd checks each host's availability by querying the host and checking the HTTP response code.

Relayd and PF

Relayd manages PF rules through the relayd anchor. At startup, relayd creates a sub-anchor for each redirection or relay it supports. These anchors are named after the `relayd.conf` statement. It also creates tables in those sub-anchors, named after the table in the rule. When you kill relayd, it pulls all of these anchors and tables from the relayd anchor.

View these anchors with pfctl(8). Here I check all anchors and sub-anchors in my PF ruleset.

```
# pfctl -sA -v
  relayd
  relayd/www
```

This shows one sub-anchor, www. It's what you'd expect if `relayd.conf` contains only the example above.

If you have multiple anchors, you might want to limit your check to only the relayd anchor and its children.

```
# pfctl -a "relayd/*" -sA
  relayd/www
```

One of the critical factors in forwarding connections is the list of hosts PF will direct traffic to. Relayd creates a table within the sub-anchor to contain exactly that. Our `relayd.conf` redirection is called www, while the table is called web. We can expect to find a sub-anchor called www containing a table called web—and indeed, we do.

```
# pfctl -a relayd/www -t web -T show
  192.0.2.101
  192.0.2.102
```

When relayd detects that a host can no longer service requests, it removes them from this table.

Now let's look at the rules relayd creates in the anchor.

```
# pfctl -a relayd/www -sr
pass in quick on rdomain 0 inet proto tcp from any to
203.0.113.213 port = 80 flags S/SA keep state
(tcp.established 600) rdr-to <www> port 80 round-robin
```

This is the only rule that appears in a roundrobin redirection. This rule should look perfectly explicable to anyone accustomed to running PF. A roundrobin redirection needs no rules for specific clients going to specific hosts, because all of the load balancing occurs within PF. Look at the last word in the PF rule: *round-robin*. PF cycles between web servers in the table for relayd.

Used without external host monitoring, PF's round-robin failover is an excellent example of fault-oblivious computing. It doesn't care if the destination server works or not, packets get sent there. With relayd to update the table of functional servers, however, PF's round-robin mode works perfectly fine. Each new connection gets forwarded to the next host in the table. Relayd pulls dysfunctional hosts from the table, and restores the entries when the host recovers.

Viewing Redirects

I always know exactly what I put in `relayd.conf`, but I'm not sure if relayd understands it as well as I do. Use relayctl(8) to see how relayd interpreted the configuration. To look specifically at redirects, use the `show redirects` subcommand.

```
# relayctl sh red
Id  Type       Name    Avlblty Status
1   redirect   smtp            down
2   redirect   www             active
3   redirect   https           active
```

This shows three active redirects: *smtp*, *www*, and *https*. Each has a unique ID number. The relayctl output shows that these are of type *redirect*, which is pretty obvious in this context but becomes more important when looking at the `show summary` subcommand. The far right column shows the status of each redirect. Redirect 1, for SMTP, is down. Redirects 2 and 3, for web services, are active and working.

To see why the SMTP redirect is down, use the `show hosts` or the `show summary` subcommand.

```
# relayctl sh ho
Id  Type   Name         Avlblty Status
1   table  smtp:587             empty
1   host   192.0.2.85   0.00%   down
    total: 0/49 checks, error: tcp read timeout
...
```

The redirect is broken because the table for this redirect is empty. The table is empty because the only host in the table is not responding to the Host Check Engine's requests. Relayd is fine; I need to go fix my mail server.

Backup Hosts

Hosts fail. Sometimes you even plan to make them fail, such as during intrusive maintenance. Relayd lets you configure *backup* hosts that take over when all of your primary hosts are down. Configure backup hosts as a second table in the redirect.

```
table <www> { 192.0.2.101 192.0.2.102 }
table <fallback> { 192.0.2.222 }

redirect www {
    listen on $ext_ip port 80
    forward to <www> check http "/" code 200
    forward to <fallback> check icmp
}
```

Our redirect has two forward statements. The first is the primary redirection target, sending traffic to hosts in the table www. The second table is the backup table, which I've called fallback. The backup hosts rely on a simple ICMP check, because if the backup is dead relayd can do absolutely nothing about it.

When your primary hosts pass the HCE checks, relayd redirects traffic to them.

So long as even one of the primary hosts in the first table function, relayd prefers a primary host. If all of the primary hosts fail, however, relayd removes all PF rules that refer to the primary hosts and starts using the backup hosts. You'll see the switch in the log and in relayctl's show redirect subcommand.

```
# relayctl sh red
Id  Type       Name  Avlblty Status
1   redirect   www           active (using backup table)
...
```

As soon as the HCE detects even one primary host ready to accept connections, it deactivates the backup hosts and re-engages the primary hosts.

Manual Failover

You can use relayctl to deliberately switch between the backup and primary host tables. You can make the backup hosts live before beginning work on your primary hosts. Enable and disable the hosts on a table-by-table basis. Start by looking at `relayctl show hosts`. I've trimmed this example for clarity.

```
# relayctl sh hosts
Id  Type   Name            Avlblty Status
1   table  www:80                  active (2 hosts)
1   host   192.0.2.101     75.61%  up
2   host   192.0.2.102     42.07%  up
2   table  fallback:80             active (1 hosts)
3   host   192.0.2.222     100.00% up
```

Our primary table is www, or table 1. Our backup table is called fallback, or table 2. Turn a table off with the `table disable` subcommand, using either the table name or the table ID number. Here I shut down the primary table.

```
# relayctl table disable 1
```

We're now running on the backup hosts.

One table can appear in multiple places in `relayd.conf`. I probably use the same table of web servers for both TLS and non-TLS services, for example. Relayctl differentiates different uses of a single table by adding the port number. Here I reactivate the primary web servers.

```
# relayctl table enable www:80
```

Once the HCE detects that the servers are able to receive traffic again, the primary table gets reactivated. How quickly this happens depends on your time settings, but the default is within 10 seconds.

Modes and Fallback Tables

Our previous examples of fallback tables use the default round-robin redirection mode on the primary table and an ICMP check on the fallback table. If you use a redirection mode other than round-robin, however, you must use the same mode on the fallback table. Here I'm using source-hash mode on the primary table, so the fallback table needs the same.

```
forward to <www> check http "/" code 200 mode source-hash
forward to <fallback> check http "/" code 200 mode source-hash
```

Relayd provides a helpful error if you use incompatible modes.

Stickiness

Complicated applications might have several TCP ports. Even older protocols like SMTP can require connections to multiple ports. Many applications expect that the client will communicate with the same host throughout a connection, and distributing the TCP/IP connections to multiple servers will confuse the issue.

The sticky-address options tells relayd to route all connections from one client to the same destination, even across multiple redirects. If you have a redirect for TLS connections, and another for non-TLS connections, sticky-address coordinates between those redirects.

```
redirect www {
    listen on $ext_ip port 80
    forward to <www> check http "/" code 200
    sticky-address
}
```

If your clients have weird issues with an application, and your application uses multiple TCP/IP ports, do some research to see if the application needs sticky addresses to properly load balance.

PF Tagging and Matching

PF can tag traffic with a label you choose, and then filter on those tags. This helps simplify complicated PF rules. If you don't know how to use tags, check a reference like Hansteen's *Book of PF* or the OpenBSD PF FAQ. Relayd lets you apply a PF tag to traffic that passes through a redirect, using the *pftag* keyword.

```
redirect www {
    listen on $ext_ip port 80
    forward to <www> check http "/" code 200
    pftag dangit
}
```

Traffic to to port 80 gets tagged with *dangit*.

Relayd defaults to creating PF rules with `pass quick`. Matching traffic passes immediately through the packet filter, without later rules getting a chance to process it. You can use the `match pftag` option to change this to only match traffic, deferring the accept/deny decision until later in the PF rules. This is commonly needed in traffic shaping.

```
redirect www {
    listen on $ext_ip port 80
    forward to <www> check http "/" code 200
    match pftag dangit
}
```

Whatever rule performs further processing on this tagged traffic needs to pass it. (Or reject it, I suppose.)

With redirects you can twist straight TCP/IP traffic any way you like. If you want to dig into the upper layers of the protocol, though, you need relays.

Chapter 13: Relays

Sometimes forwarding TCP/IP isn't enough. You need the load balancer to dig into the traffic, examining protocol headers and scrutinizing contents. Deep inspection is built on top of packet filtering, but needs more than a handful of PF rules. The client traffic needs to terminate at relayd, and relayd needs to initiate its own connection to the destination server. Relayd reads traffic from the client and the server, performs its inspections and transformations, and hands the result to other party. This kind of load balancing is often called an *application layer gateway*, a *proxy server*, or some variant on these, but relayd calls it a *relay* because the OpenBSD folks don't have time for or patience with those lengthy names.

Relays let you manipulate traffic in a whole bunch of ways. But let's start with the simplest case.

Relays versus Redirects

Here's a very simple relay for a cluster of two web servers.

```
table <www> { 192.0.2.101 192.0.2.102 }
relay www {
    listen on 203.0.113.213 port 80
    forward to <www> port http check http "/" code 200
}
```

This relay, called *www*, has a farm of two web servers. There's a listen statement, telling relayd which IP and port relayd accepts traffic for. The forward statement tells relayd where to send that traffic. The Host Check Engine uses the same check as a redirect would.

157

With this relay in place, web requests get relayed to the hosts and the hosts respond, exactly as they would for a redirect. So what's the difference?

First, take a look at the open TCP ports on the relayd host. When you're using a redirect, relayd does not open any ports on the load balancer. With a relay, though, the load balancer has an open port.

```
$ netstat -na -f inet
...
tcp  0  0  203.0.113.213.80  *.*  LISTEN
...
```

Relayd is accepting TCP connections on port 80. If you open up a packet sniffer on the web server, you'll see that the incoming requests all come from the relayd server rather than the original client. This protects your server against TCP/IP-level attacks. Yes, the load balancer still has to face those attacks, but an OpenBSD host will withstand those attacks far better than a commercial operating system like Windows or Red Hat.

Now take a look at the PF rules. The relayd anchor has no sub-anchors, no tables, and no rules. Relayd is doing all the work itself. While this simplifies managing anchors, it does mean that there's no PF rule to allow access to the relay. You must add rules for permitted relays to /etc/pf.conf. Normally, this means opening access to the port and IP the relay listens on.

Active Relays and Sessions

Use relayctl(8) to view the running relays, the hosts in those relays, and the currently running sessions. Start by viewing relays with the show relays subcommand.

```
# relayctl sh rel
Id  Type    Name  Avlblty Status
1   relay   www           active
    total: 8 sessions
    last: 0/60s 8/h 8/d sessions
    average: 0/60s 0/h 0/d sessions
```

Our test relayd instance has one running relay. It's called www, and it's active. If you've been paying attention, none of this should surprise you.

Beneath the relay we get statistics on what the relay has processed. This particular relay has handled eight sessions. The *last* line shows how many sessions it's handled in the previous sixty seconds (zero), the previous hour (eight), and the previous day (also eight). The next line gives average load per sixty seconds, hour, and day. As you can tell, I don't work my test lab very hard.

A relay *session* is a single client request to a server. If you have ten requests passing through a relay, you have ten active sessions. Relayd keeps its own state table for each session, much as PF does for each live TCP/IP connection. To view all of the sessions relayd is currently tracking, use the show sessions subcommand.

```
# relayctl sh ses
session 0:1 198.51.100.70:52835 -> 192.0.2.101:80
RUNNING
    age 00:00:11, idle 00:00:01, relay 1, pid 68504
```

We have one session, number 0. It's connecting the client's IP 198.51.100.70 to the host 192.0.2.101, and is actively running. This session has been running for 11 seconds and been idle for one second. Finally, it's attached to relay number 1, running under the relayd process with PID 68504.

Our simple example isn't very interesting, though. Relays become interesting with the introduction of protocols.

Relayd Filters

Relayd includes the ability to filter, and change traffic. A filter is a series of statements, processed in order. Each statement contains rules to block, pass, or modify traffic. The modification might be "pass the traffic to another server," as in our example above, or it might be "throw this away and use something else." Stacking these statements lets you achieve effects like "Send all IPv4 traffic to this server and all IPv6 to this other server."

Filters normally appear in protocol statements, which then get applied to relays. Each filter statement has the following format.

```
action parameters
```

The action is what the filter does—permits the traffic, blocks the traffic, or performs some other action. The parameters can define the traffic that the statement applies to or change a setting. Yes, this is a minimal example, but don't worry. You'll see a mind-numbing number of examples before this chapter ends.

Filters go inside protocols.

Relayd Protocols

Relayd includes protocols for handling common Internet traffic. It has tools to sanitize DNS queries, adjust HTTP and HTTPS traffic, and alter TCP sessions. The main function of protocols is to apply filters, letting you adapt, modify, and block application traffic. We'll discuss each of these separately.

Here's a relay with a simple protocol and filter.

```
tcp protocol fixup {
   tcp nodelay
}
relay ssh {
   listen on 203.0.113.213 port 2222
   forward to <ssh> port 22
   protocol fixup
}
```

Protocol definitions must appear in `relayd.conf` before any relays or redirections. Any protocols defined after the first relay or redirection become invisible to relayd. If you get a `no such protocol` error and you're really certain the protocol appears in the configuration, make sure that the protocol appears sufficiently early in the configuration file.

The first entry is a TCP protocol called *fixup*. Relayd's TCP protocol includes several options, which we'll discuss later, but the important thing here is that this protocol includes a filter with one statement: *tcp nodelay*.

We then define a relay, called *ssh*. This relay listens on an IP address and port, just like any other relay, and it forwards the connection to the next host in the table of ssh servers. The new bit is the last line, where we apply the protocol fixup to this relay.

In combination, this example means "Proxy SSH connections, and apply the TCP_NODELAY option to created TCP connections." Using SSH without TCP_NODELAY is incredibly annoying.

Relayd supports three protocols: tcp, dns, and http.

The *tcp* protocol is the default. It allows you to apply a TCP filter to a relay. If you don't specify the kind of protocol you're defining, relayd assumes it's a tcp protocol.

The *dns* protocol is specifically for UDP-based DNS queries. It randomizes request IDs to help protect against spoofed responses. DNS also uses TCP, but the request ID randomization isn't needed there.

The *http* protocol lets you apply filters based on HTTP characteristics. You can pass, block, or tweak traffic based on HTTP factors like cookies, headers, HTTP methods, and more.

There is no generic UDP protocol. UDP is designed for applications that want their own protocols. Relayd can't guess what each application wants.[26]

Each relay applies exactly one protocol.

Configuring the protocols is pretty simple. All the logic is in the filters. We'll spend a whole bunch of time on filters, starting with TCP.

TCP Filters

Applications can request that the kernel create TCP connections with special options, so that TCP can accommodate the application protocol. Some applications need selective acknowledgements, or choke with bundling requests, or need extra large window sizes. When relayd uses a redirection to distribute traffic, the client and server handle these settings on their own. When using a relay, however, your relayd system accepts the client's requests and creates a new connection to reach the server. Any special TCP requests need to be made by relayd, and relayd has a whole bunch of options for TCP tuning.

You can include multiple TCP options in a single protocol definition by placing each on its own line.

```
tcp protocol fixup {
   tcp nodelay
   tcp sack
   tcp backlog 128
}
```

If you prefer, you can give the tcp keyword and list all of the options within brackets.

```
tcp protocol fixup {
   tcp { sack, nodelay, backlog 128 }
}
```

26   Feel free to write your own filter for, say, UDP-based NFS traffic, and submit it to OpenBSD. They can use a laugh.

TCP is the default protocol type. You can drop it entirely from the protocol name.

```
protocol fixup {
  …
```

Use whatever you find more readable.

While relayd supports a bunch of options, don't go spraying them around willy-nilly. Many applications function just fine without TCP tuning. Rely on your application vendor's documentation, or perform some Internet searches to see if your application behaves weirdly with load balancers. Don't change the TCP options and hope they'll fix things.

The common TCP protocol options and their effects are identical to the options available in httpd, as discussed in Chapter 7. Go look there for details on the options *backlog, ip minttl, ip ttl, nodelay, sack,* and *socket buffer.*

We'll apply these options to filters for other protocols.

The Relayd DNS Protocol

Relayd does not include a generic UDP protocol adjuster. The UDP network protocol is stateless and is used in all sorts of weird, unconnected ways. Relayd does include a protocol for UDP-based DNS queries, because DNS is a well-defined protocol and relayd can do a few things to help protect the integrity of DNS queries with these clients. Start by defining a table for your DNS servers.

```
table <dns> { 192.0.2.101 192.0.2.102 }
```

Now define an instance of the DNS protocol. I've called this one "dnsfix."

```
dns protocol dnsfix
```

DNS queries can run over either TCP or UDP, so relayd must listen on both protocols.

```
relay dns {
    listen on 203.0.113.213 port 53
    forward to <dns> check tcp
    protocol dnsfix
}
```

Chapter 11 gives a check script for DNS servers. Why not use it? This kind of relay is most useful for protecting queries leaving your network. The check script is for your own authoritative nameservers.

Filter Essentials

Filters support basic operators that can be shared across many protocols. The only protocol they're really useful for right now is HTTP, but they could be used for other protocols in the future. Our examples will focus on HTTP.

HTTP filters can quickly become complicated, but only because HTTP is complicated. Relayd's http filters include the ability to match on HTTP methods, cookies, headers, URL, and more. They get much longer than filters for TCP traffic, as this snippet of the sample `relayd.conf` included with relayd shows.

```
…
# Block disallowed sites
match request label "URL filtered!"
block request quick url "www.example.com/" value "*"

# Block disallowed browsers
match request label "Please try a <em>different Browser</em>"
block request quick header "User-Agent" \
    value "Mozilla/4.0 (compatible; MSIE *"

# Block some well-known Instant Messengers
match request label "Instant messenger disallowed!"
block response quick header "Content-Type" \
    value "application/x-msn-messenger"
…
```

This filter blocks three different types of HTTP traffic. The first chunk filters out the host www.example.com. The second detects browsers that have a specific User-Agent header and blocks them. The last blocks a certain internet chat client.

Some filter parameters (such as request, label, and quick) are available to any protocol. The only existing relayd protocol that can use these parameters is httpd, but more protocols could be written in the future and they could take advantage of these parameters. Other filter parameters (like method, header, and cookie) are only available for the HTTP protocol in particular.

We'll start with the generic parameters and proceed into the HTTP-only options. As this book was published, though, these generic parameters are only applicable to HTTP filters.

Filter Action

Filters for HTTP traffic start with block, match, pass, return, tcp, or tls.

A *block* statement prevents traffic that matches the statement from passing through the filter. We saw three examples of this in the previous section.

The *match* statement inflicts some change on traffic that matches the parameters. As you can see, those parameters can be extensive.

The *pass* statement says to let the traffic through. Filters default to allowing traffic, so pass is normally used to grant a narrow exception to a broad block.

The *return* statement tells the filter to return an error to the client. Relayd normally drops blocked traffic silently. We'll use return statements in "Returning Errors" later this chapter.

A *tcp* statement adjusts TCP parameters, exactly like a TCP filter.

Finally, *tls* statements let you add, remove, or filter on TLS characteristics. We cover TLS in Chapter 14.

Once you define the action, you can assign parameters.

Requests and Responses

When you bring relayd into the mix, the data flow suddenly looks more complicated. The client initiates a TCP/IP connection to the relay. The relay fiddles and twiddles the request and initiates a TCP/IP connection to the application server. The application server sends its response to the relayd host, which might do more fiddling, then sends the modified response back to the client. Relayd offers "request" and "response" as filter parameters, but which request and response, exactly, will it affect?

The *request* parameter applies to the client's connection to the relayd host. If you're checking for a specific header in the client request, use the request parameter. Relayd can add or remove details from the request.

The *response* parameter applies to the application server's response to the client. The relay sits in the middle of that response.

Used alone, request and response parameters make poor filters. The following filter is perfectly legit, but not terribly useful.

```
http protocol daft {
   block response
}

relay www {
   listen on 203.0.113.213 port 80
   forward to <www> port http check http "/" code 200
   protocol daft
}
```

This relay filter permits requests, but blocks responses. Put this filter into place in your test environment and try to call up a web page. The web server's log shows the requests arriving. A packet sniffer shows the responses leaving the web server and arriving at the relay. The web browser will report an error, though, because relayd refuses to pass the response along.

Stopping traffic is pretty straightforward. Let's stop traffic a little more politely.

Providing Errors

When relayd refuses traffic it does so silently. The user gets no error message. Depending on your configuration, error messages might leak security information. You can use the *return error* parameter to turn on error messages. Include this parameter inside your protocol.

```
http protocol daft {
   return error
   block response
}
```

Rather than a browser error, relayd returns an appropriate error message to the client. In the case of a web browser, it's a 403 Forbidden error, with the server's IP address and port.

As this is OpenBSD, however, the error page is bright red with white Comic Sans text. The *style* parameter lets you define a CSS style to be applied to the error page. Put your style sheet in quotes. Adding a new style sheet overrides relayd's default style sheet, though, so be certain to include all desirable formatting in your new CSS.

```
http protocol daft {
   return error style "body { background: #a00000; \
      color: lightblue; font-family: 'Comic Sans MS' ; }"
   block response
}
```

Remember to use single quotes inside your CSS, or escape your double quotes.

Individual statements can provide custom error messages to be fed to the return statement. Use the *label* option to set the error. The client displays the label as per the protocol, so in this case, we can use HTML.

167

```
http protocol daft {
   return error
   block response label \
      "<h1>blame @billallaire73. For EVERYTHING.</h1>"
}
```

As relayd defaults to not providing error messages, the users will know only what you tell them. Which is as it should be.

Logical Operators

These parameters are most commonly used to help make decisions within more detailed protocols. Combined with block, pass, and match, you can control exactly what types of data traverse your relay. We'll see many examples of these throughout the HTTP protocol discussion.

The *inet* and *inet6* options match connections that use IPv4 or IPv6. Mostly, you'll pass connections along in the protocol they arrive in.

The *quick* parameter stops filter processing. Relayd immediately blocks or passes this traffic. We'll use this a whole bunch, starting in "HTTP Methods" later this chapter.

The *no* option turns off an option that was turned on earlier. Maybe you set a label early in the filter, but a subset of your traffic doesn't need that label. Set that label globally, then remove it from that smaller group in a later statement.

The *tag* parameter adds a named tag to traffic that matches this statement. If you understand PF tags, you understand relayd tags. You can add a tag to matching traffic, and then pass, reject, or modify all traffic with that tag.

Really using these logical operators requires a protocol to muck with. Without further ado, let's dive into HTTP.

HTTP Filter Essentials

Here's the good stuff. Filtering HTTP traffic lets you use and abuse arbitrary web characteristics such as the HTTP method, cookies, headers, query string, and so on to alter, block, and permit traffic.

While relayd has many tools for abusing web traffic, that doesn't mean you should use them. Filters are necessary for specific relay operations. Some filters might work to protect your application against specific attacks or shore up weaknesses. Most HTTP applications need the features they use, though. If you're stuck trying to cope with an application misfeature, though, a filter might just save the day.

Let's look at methods first.

HTTP Methods

You've probably heard of the GET and PUT requests. These are examples of HTTP *methods*. A method is how a client requests the server do something. "Give me this thing." "Take this thing." "Attach me to a resource named BillIsADoof." Web applications are usually built on a few different methods, but HTTP includes a whole bunch of methods. People add more methods all the time. Relayd recognizes a couple dozen methods and will let you filter on them using the *method* option and the name of the method.

This lets us build our first logic in a filter. Web developer Bill assures me that his application only uses the GET method. I get him to tell me that in email, then disallow all other methods.

```
http protocol getonly {
    return error
    pass quick method GET
    block label "Forbidden Method"
}
```

The first line inside this filter displays error messages.

The second line is our first piece of filter logic we'll study. It's a `pass` statement with the `quick` keyword, which means that any matching traffic is immediately allowed without going further down the filter. It matches anything with the method GET. This filter immediately passes GET requests.

The last line is a block. It offers an error, "Forbidden Method." Everything except an HTTP GET winds up here.[27]

Permitting additional methods means adding additional `pass quick` lines.

Configuring Matches

HTTP methods are a single word and easy to check for. They're right near the front of the request. Other parts of the HTTP protocol are a little more complicated. Some, like a web site's URL, can have a long and complicated format. You might need many of these in your configuration file. Relayd lets you match based on a value set in *relayd.conf*, values from a file, or the hash of a value.

We'll use URLs as an example. We haven't yet discussed the intricacies of URL matching, but if you're reading this book you probably already have a vague idea that filtering sites by URL is a thing.

You can explicitly define matching terms in *relayd.conf*. Here's a filter statement to block access to a particular domain name.

```
block request url "www.mallard.info/"
```

This works fine to match one or two sites, but maintaining lengthy blacklists in *relayd.conf* gets painful. You might need an automatically updated blacklist, which is most easily maintained in an external file. Use the file option and the path to the file, in quotes.

```
block request url file "/etc/blocklist.txt"
```

---

27   The vital thing here is to save Bill's email, so that when he complains about the error I can show him it's his own fault.

Items in the text file must be formatted exactly as they would in `relayd.conf`. Relayd reads this file only at startup or at reload.

Finally, you can give the SHA1 or MD5 digest or hash of the item to be matched. Sometimes, using the hash is simpler than including a long horrible HTTP protocol detail, such as mile-long headers or cookies. It also might be simpler than trying to quote escape the weird characters increasingly common in web applications.

```
block request url digest e0938cef9ad...
```

Relayd determines which hash you're using by the length of the hash. SHA1 hashes are 40 characters, while MD5 are 32 characters.

Compute the hash of a string like so.

```
$ echo -n "www.mallard.info/" | sha1
```

Relayd strips up to five components from the front and back of the request path when performing the comparison, to get rid of arguments and alternate hostnames and such.

While relayd can filter on values set by any of these methods, the examples in this book use plain text directly in `relayd.conf` to improve the chances you'll understand just what we're doing.

Key/Value Matches

Every web request has a URL. Other HTTP settings—like cookies, headers, and query strings—include a key and a value. Sometimes you care only about the presence of an item, and want to filter on the traffic if the item is even present.

```
action request item "variable"
```

Maybe we're looking for the HTTP header X-Bill. If the header is present, we want to block the request.

```
 block request header "X-Bill"
```

171

The presence alone might not be enough, though. HTTP headers have values. You might only care about this request if the header has a particular value. This means expanding the filter syntax with the *value* keyword. Using value lets you check the contents of a query, or other variable, like so.

```
block request item "variable" value "value"
```

Suppose we want to block requests with the X-Bill header, but only if they're set to a particular value.

```
block request header "X-Bill" value "competent"
```

With that, let's see what you can do to the innards of HTTP traffic.

Filtering the Web

Relayd lets you filter based on a whole bunch of different web traffic characteristics. These include the site URL, cookies, the request path, the contents of the query string, and HTTP headers. Filtering on URL, cookies, path, and query string only work in requests. You can filter HTTP headers in both requests and responses.

URLs are the most obvious, so we'll start there.

Matching URLs

Uniform Resource Locators, or URLs, are the most obvious part of a web site. A URL is the complete location of a web site, including the domain name, the path after the first slash, and all the stuff with question marks and equal signs at the end. Relayd can filter by URL. This capability is most useful when using relayd as an outbound proxy, as we'll discuss in Chapter 15, but it might help protect your application as well.

Relayd can match a URL based on part or all of a domain name. This is a literal match, without any shell globs or patterns or regexes or any variables. (You can put wildcards like * in `relayd.conf`, but they won't work.) The URL must be in quotes, and must include at least one slash.

Suppose you have a web site that's only for internal use, and shouldn't be accessible to the outside world. Use *url* as a match term and give the site in quotes. Make certain you include at least one slash.

```
block request url "www4.mallard.info/" label "GET OUT"
```

This blocks any pages on that server.

Or maybe Developer Bill insists he really needs a web interface for his database, and he promises that he'll restrict access to it at the web server. You could block the outside world's access to that interface through the relay.

```
block request url "www4.mallard.info/phpMyAdmin" \
  label "Bill is a Wimp"
```

URL matching searches to see if a site matches the URL block by stripping up to five terms off the front and back of the URL. A block on mallard.info also blocks www.mallard.info, www4.mallard.info, test.www9.mallard.info, and all pages under any of these. Blocking more than five layers of directories in a site requires code changes or more specific block statements.

Matching Queries

A query string is everything in the URL after the first question mark. Web applications use query strings to set variables.[28] Relayd lets you pick out individual query terms and act on their values.

Suppose Developer Bill has a debugging mode in his web application. He activates debugging mode by adding the query terms debug=yes to the URL. I don't want people outside our organization to get access to debugging mode. Use the *query* option and the query term you want to block.

---

28   Bad web applications use query strings to hold sensitive information.

```
block request query "debug"
```

The mere presence of the debug query term blocks the request.

Eventually, Bill wants to allow certain customers to open pages in debugging mode. He's created a special debug mode that only shows certain information, controlled by setting the query term *debug* to *customer*. He wants me to allow this through the relay. More importantly, the boss wants me to allow this through the relay, so I guess I have to.

We need to break out the value keyword. For our use, the query variable is *debug* and the value we want to accept is *customer*.

```
block request query debug
pass request query "debug" value "customer"
```

We block the query variable "debug" globally. The second statement permits the query variable "debug" if and only if it's set to "customer."

Request Path

Relayd can filter on the request path, also known as "everything after the domain name." If you make a request to https://www.mallard.info/status.php?a=b, the request path is *status.php?a=b*.

To configure a request path in `relayd.conf`, chop it into two parts. Everything before that first question mark is the key you're searching for. The remaining part, the query string, is the value. Here I block our example request path.

```
block request path "/status.php" value "a=b"
```

The request path needs to start with a slash, and the query string must be an exact match.

Both terms can accept shell globs. Here I block any page that begins with *status*, and any query string than includes variables that begin with *a*.

```
block request path "/status*" value "a*=b"
```

Relayd is sensitive to order. If you list a complicated query string with many variables, the variables must appear in exactly that order in the browser. A user can modify the query string before sending the request. Only the malicious users will bother. Don't rely on filtering long query strings for access control; you're better off matching individual query terms.

Cookies

People get paranoid about cookies. Web sites have cookie policies. Maybe your company promises that your site will never, ever use cookies. Cookie filtering only works in requests, so you can't prevent your web developer from using them. You can prevent the client from returning those cookies to your server, though, which is almost as good. Use the *cookie* keyword. Here we unilaterally block cookies.

```
block request cookie "*"
```

You can more selectively filter on cookies by giving the cookie name. Many web sites use a cookie called persistent_login to keep users logged in. Perhaps your app shouldn't be using that cookie. Block it.

```
block request cookie "persistent_login*"
```

If you have not only a particular cookie name to filter on, but a specific value for that cookie, include that too. The real world value is probably much longer than this one.

```
block request cookie "persistent_login*" value \
  "whatever"
```

If you're filtering on cookies, though, you're probably solving the wrong problem.

Headers

HTTP headers carry a whole bunch of information about an application. Applications use all sorts of headers. They're a great candidate for filters. Most users can't see HTTP headers without a browser plug-in or a packet sniffer.

Match on a particular header by using the *header* keyword.

```
block request header "Upgrade"
```

If you want to match not only the header, but a specific value of that header, add the value parameter and the target value.

```
block request header "Upgrade" value "websocket"
```

Bill swears his web app doesn't use websockets. We'll see.

You can now pass and block HTTP traffic based on its protocol characteristics. What about modifying, though?

Modifying HTTP Headers

Passing and blocking traffic is kind of boring. Mucking with the contents of traffic is much more interesting. HTTP controls most of its behavior through headers. Relayd gives great flexibility creating, removing, and changing headers. Modify traffic with the set, append, and remove options.

Set

The *set* option sets an item's value. Use this to change the value of a HTTP header, a query string, a URL, or anything else relayd can filter on. If the thing doesn't exist, it gets added. The set option is most commonly used with the match operation.

Here I change the Connection header. This header controls if the TCP/IP connection should stay open once the request is granted, or if it should terminate. Many applications set this to keep-alive even if they don't need it. Here, we tell relayd to rewrite the incoming client request and to make this header always say close.

```
match request header set "Connection" value "close"
```

The client can ask for any Connection header it likes. We aren't listening.

If the requested header doesn't exist, relayd adds it to the request.

You can also use the set option with a response, to send extra headers back to the client. If you need to do this, though, it's a good reason to go slap your web developer.[29]

Append

The *append* option adds another header to the request. Your relay shouldn't strip out existing versions of the header, but only add its own information. You'll see this when a request traverses multiple proxy servers. Use append to add your own information without destroying existing info.

Append statements most often need dynamic information. See "Header Macros" later this chapter for examples of append statements.

If the header does not exist, append creates it.

You'll especially need this when forwarding TLS requests, as we'll see in Chapter 14.

Remove

If you don't want a particular header traversing the relay, use the *remove* option to rip it out of the request. Most client request headers are absolutely necessary for proper web application function, but web developer Bill ate the last slice of cold pizza this morning.

```
match request header remove "User-Agent"
```

I'll explain it was a typo, and I'll fix it while he orders more pizza.

---

29   Again.

You could also be more specific, stripping only headers with certain values. Here I strip the Server header from replies, but only if the value is "Apache 2.4."

```
match response header remove "Server" value "Apache 2.4"
```

Why would I possibly want to do this? I have no idea, but Bill will certainly offer me reason one day.

Header Macros

Relayd includes a set of macros to create dynamic headers. These let you pass information to a client or the web server that relayd would otherwise obscure. Web development tools like PHP can extract header information.

A relay is not a NAT. The client and the web server both connect to the relayd host. Relayd provides macros that let you pass IP information to the other end of the connection. When used with a request, $REMOTE_PORT and $REMOTE_ADDR give the client's IP address and the source port.

```
match request header set "X-Client-IP" \
    value "$REMOTE_ADDR:$REMOTE_PORT"
```

Relayd adds the TCP/IP information to the request header.

The $REMOTE_PORT and $REMOTE_ADDR macros behave differently with responses, however. They pass the server's actual IP and the connection's destination port through to the client. If you're using relayd and PF to protect and manage your server farm, leaking this information is probably undesirable.

You can also pass the IP address and port of the relay through to your server, using the $SERVER_ADDR and $SERVER_PORT macros. This can help your application differentiate if, say, this request comes from the public Internet or your office. You'll need both remote and server information in headers to forward TLS connections.

```
match request header append "X-Forwarded-For" \
   value "$REMOTE_ADDR"
match request header append "X-Forwarded-By" \
   value "$SERVER_ADDR:$SERVER_PORT"
```

Finally, $SERVER_NAME gives the name of the relay software. This is normally "OpenBSD relayd." And $TIMEOUT gives the number of seconds for an idle relay's state to time out.

You can now filter and manipulate web traffic with relayd. But filters can also feed information back into relayd.

Relayd Logging

Someone will inevitable ask you "what did the relay do to me?" You'll want logs to determine that.

Relayd can send only updates to the log, or can log all updates and changes. Logging filter effects requires the `log all` option in `relayd.conf`, or enabling complete logging with relayctl(8). Log messages appear in `/var/log/daemon`.

Log a filter statement by adding the *log* option. The log option goes after you state what you're filtering, but before the value.

```
block request url log "www.mallard.info/phpMyAdmin"
```

Not all statements accept the log option. You'll have to try it and see if it works for you.

Feeding Hashes

Certain load balancing methods used by relays can accept information from the flow of HTTP data, as discussed in Chapter 11. Use a filter statement and the *hash* option to identify traffic that you want relayd to feed to the load balancing algorithm.

Options like IP addresses, HTTP headers, cookies, and the like really aren't suitable for feeding load balancing algorithms. The most common choice is some sort of session ID. This means each client gets treated individually, even when you have multiple browsers running on the same client computer. Session IDs are normally set in query strings, using a variable like `sessid`. Here I identify that variable in the query and feed it to the load balancer.

```
match query hash "sessid"
```

This give the best load balancing randomness you can hope for.

Now that you have a grip on relayd's filtering abilities, let's use those abilities to play games with TLS.

Chapter 14: TLS and Acceleration

A relay accepts TCP/IP connections, filters or transforms the request, and sends a new request on to the target. Nothing says that the new connection made by relayd needs to use the same protocol used by the original request. Relayd includes special support for adding and stripping TLS from network requests. You can use relayd to add TLS to an unencrypted protocol, or strip TLS from a network request. That ancient web server that can't handle TLS but that supports a mission-critical security-sensitive application? Put a relay in front of it and add TLS there. You can add TLS to any TCP connection, even on protocols that don't have a TLS version.

Relayd can act as a TLS server, a TLS client, or both.

When a client makes a TLS connection to your relay, your relay acts as a TLS server. The client browser reads the certificate provided by your relay and processes it as it would any other certificate. The relay forwards the connection to another host. You decide if that new connection needs TLS or not. A relay running in server mode is called an *SSL accelerator* or *TLS accelerator*, and is commonly used to provide TLS to a non-TLS service.

When TLS makes a TLS connection to another host, it acts as a *TLS client*. Whatever connection it's forwarding gets wrapped in TLS. If the client connected to the relay without TLS, relayd will wrap the service in TLS. If whatever's at the destination doesn't speak TLS natively, you can stick a TLS accelerator in front of it to provide decryption.

When your relay accepts and sends TLS connections, it's performing *TLS inspection*. The connection is encrypted coming to the relay, and it's encrypted when it leaves the relay, but inside the relay it's unencrypted. You can filter a client request any way you desire, then wrap it back up in TLS and send it on to the original destination. You'll most often see TLS inspection used in an organization's Internet proxy.

TLS imposes specific protocol requirements. Web requests made through TLS use additional HTTP headers, which you'll need to add or remove. Acting as a TLS server means using a TLS certificate. Performing TLS inspection means you not only need a TLS certificate, but you need to run a certificate authority recognized by the client.

We'll start by building our own TLS accelerator. Start with your certificate.

TLS Certificates and Relayd

The good news is that thanks to Let's Encrypt, TLS certificates are now free. More good news is that you don't have to tell a relay where to find the certificate and its private key. The bad news is, you don't have to configure it because relayd expects you to place the key and the certificate in a specific location.

Certificate files go in `/etc/ssl`, while the private keys for those certs go in `/etc/ssl/private`. Each file needs to be named in a very specific format: the IP address of the relay, a colon, the port the relay is listening on, a period, and either `.crt` or `.key`. Consider the following relay configuration from `/etc/relayd.conf`.

```
relay "www4ssl" {
    listen on 203.0.113.213 port 443 with tls
    protocol www4ssl
    forward to <www>
}
```

This relay listens on port 443 on the IP 203.0.113.213. The *with tls* option tells relayd to use TLS on this port. Place the site certificate in the file `/etc/ssl/203.0.113.213:443.crt`, and the private key in `/etc/ssl/private/203.0.113.213:443.key`. If relayd does not find these files, it complains and dies.

If the certificate and key for a relay don't exist, relayd checks for files named after the IP but without the port. This means that you want to use the same certificate for all ports on the relay host, you can skip the port number in the filename. For example, suppose you're running relays on ports 587 and 995 and you want them both to use the same certificate. Place their certificate in `/etc/ssl/203.0.113.213.crt` and their private key in `/etc/ssl/private/203.0.113.213.key`. A certificate named after a port gets priority, though—your files named after port 443 get used for port 443 even when the generic fallback exists.

TLS Acceleration Protocols

TLS requests behave a little differently on the network than unencrypted requests. Many applications expect headers identifying who forwarded the request and where the request originated. Certain TCP options pretty clearly improve performance. OpenBSD ships an example `relayd.conf` with a suitable TLS acceleration filter, but as I'll be modifying this filter to handle additional problems, we'll go through it here.

```
http protocol https {
  match request header append "X-Forwarded-For" \
    value "$REMOTE_ADDR"
  match request header append "X-Forwarded-By" \
    value "$SERVER_ADDR:$SERVER_PORT"

  match request header set "Connection" value "close"

  # Various TCP performance options
  tcp { nodelay, sack, socket buffer 65536, \
    backlog 128 }
}
```

No matter what, we append our relay host's information to the X-Forwarded-For and X-Forwarded-By headers. If the application doesn't need these headers, their presence won't hurt anything.

The sample `relayd.conf` always changes the Connection header to *close*. This tells the server to answer a single HTTP request per TCP connection. The alternative, *keep-alive*, tells the server to answer several HTTP requests in a single TCP connection. Putting everything in a single TCP connection decreases the networking overhead, but puts all the load on a single back-end server. Closing the connection with every request increases the networking overhead but spreads it between all of the servers in the farm. Test your application with and without close.[30]

The TCP options shown are useful for TLS connections, and you should probably use them. As always, though, measure their impact in the real world.

Relay Certs

One relay can support dozens or hundreds of web sites. A relay performing TLS acceleration can also support dozens or hundreds of sites, but adds a few complications.

---

30   I want to say "never blindly copy and paste examples," but if you haven't learned that by now I'm can't help you.

The accelerator wraps whatever site you request in the TLS certificate you provide. If the certificate does not list one of the sites behind the relay, though, HTTPS requests for that site will generate an error. My TLS accelerator has two sites behind it, www.mallard.info and www4.mallard.info. My TLS cert lists only one domain, www4.mallard.info. While there are no links pointing to a TLS version of www.mallard.info, anyone that happens to try it will get an error.

If you're using ACME for free TLS certificates, the simplest fix is to make sure that all of the sites on your web server are listed in the certificate. When you're using ACME, make sure you use the full chain certificate file as the certificate.

Creating and renewing the TLS cert on the web host means that you need a process to copy the TLS certs from the web host to the load balancer.

Another obvious solution might seem to be adding to a filter to turn off access to the non-TLS sites over the TLS relay, but the client must negotiate a TLS session before it can receive the error. The user would need to add a TLS exception to view the site before getting the error that she couldn't view the site.

Modifying TLS Requests

You can dictate how a relayd protocol will create and handle TLS sessions. Many of the TLS options from Chapter 6 work within a relayd protocol. Most of these should only be used by people very familiar with cryptography, and those folks know better than to mess with them. I'll discuss the most commonly used options here.

You might need to refuse certain TLS versions or require a specific TLS version, or even permit old-fashioned SSL. Relayd defaults to accepting only TLS version 1.2; if you want older versions you'll need to enable them. You can specify TLS versions individually as *tlsv1.0* and *tlsv1.1*. SSLv3 is available with the option *sslv3*.

```
tls {sslv3, tls1.0, tls1.1}
```

The option *no tlsv1.2* disables TLS 1.2, while the *tlsv1* option includes all supported versions of TLS.

A TLS server and client normally negotiate on which cryptographic algorithms they will use, each working from a list of preferred options. The *no cipher-server-preference* option turns off relayd's list of preferences, letting the client pick any supported algorithm.

Relayd supports TLS session tickets, as per RFC 5077. Stateless session tickets break a very few applications. If you need to turn them off, use the option *no session tickets*.

Sometimes a client thinks it needs to renegotiate a TLS session. This can lead to a denial of service attack on the server, so it's disabled by default. To permit the client to initiate renegotiating a TLS session, set the option *client-renegotiation*.

Finally, you can set a named list of ciphers that this TLS filter supports. We discussed these cipher lists briefly in Chapter 6, but the default (HIGH:!aNULL) is perfectly fine for almost everyone. Mess with the cipher list, or the options that let you choose elliptic curves and Diffie-Hellman parameters, at your own peril.

Relayd provides just about everything you'll need to protect your site. Now let's turn it inside out.

Chapter 15: Relayd as Outbound Proxy

Many organizations use PF to provide and control Internet service to their users. PF makes a good general-purpose TCP/IP access control tool, but sometimes you need something that can look higher up the protocol stack. Relayd's relays can fill that role—after all, the Internet is nothing but a really big server farm maintained by other people. Unlike more traditional proxies like Squid, relayd leverages some really clever PF features to intercept traffic.

Relayd is not a perfect outbound proxy. It's flexible and powerful, but some edge cases give it trouble. Be sure you understand relayd's limitations before deploying it across your enterprise!

PF Diversion versus Redirection

PF has two ways to steer packets: divert-to and rdr-to.

Redirection with a *rdr-to* statement changes where a packet goes, but it does so by rewriting the packet's destination address and (probably) the ports. Redirection is normally used for incoming connections, such as a server hidden behind a NAT device.

Diversion is a newer method of packet interception, written in part to address shortcomings of redirection for certain situations. Using a *divert-to* statement steers incoming connections to a local port and address without modifying the packets. The client thinks it has connected to the actual remote host, when really it's connected to a port on the relayd host.

Diversion is the common way to proxy with relayd, and it's what I'll use in examples. I will mention where you'd need changes for redirection, but we won't go too deeply into that.

Configuring a Proxy Host

An OpenBSD host serving as an outbound proxy needs a configuration much like that discussed in Chapter 9. It's not exactly identical to an inbound relay, however, so we need to go through it. I'll refer back to concepts covered in Chapter 9 to reduce the annoying repetition as much as possible.

This host has two network interfaces. One faces the public Internet and is part of the group egress. The other faces inside and is part of the group office.

We start `pf.conf` with basic protections, defining management workstations and external DNS servers, and traffic sanitization. Remember, relays don't use the PF anchor, so we won't include it in our ruleset. (You will need the anchor if you're using also using redirects.)

```
include "/etc/rfc5735.conf"
mgmt="{203.0.113.70 198.51.100.0/24}"
dns="{8.8.8.8 8.8.4.4}"
set loginterface egress
set block-policy return
set skip on lo0
match in all scrub (no-df random-id max-mss 1440)
```

Next we configure NAT for our inside network with a *match* statement, but don't permit any traffic. We block all traffic from known bogus networks, put in our default deny rule, and allow the proxy itself to initiate any connections needed.

```
match out on egress inet from !(egress:network) to any
nat-to (egress:0)
block in quick on egress from <rfc5735> to any
block in quick on egress from any to <rfc5735>
block all
pass out quick inet
```

What can the hosts inside do? We'll let them have DNS to our DNS servers. They can also use ping and traceroute. And that's everything.

```
pass in on inside proto { tcp udp } from \
  (inside:network) to $dns port 53
pass in on inside proto icmp from (inside:network) \
  to (inside)
pass in proto udp to port 33433 >< 33626
```

What can the outside world do? We'll give them ping and traceroute as well, plus let our external management workstations get in.

```
pass in on egress proto icmp from any to (egress)
pass in on egress proto udp to port 33433 >< 33626
pass in on egress from $mgmt
```

Rules permitting access to a relay should go at the very end of this configuration.

For NAT, you must enable packet forwarding with the `net.inet.ip.forwarding` sysctl.

Rules permitting access to a configured relay go at the end of the configuration. Often, though, you won't need them.

The First Outbound Proxy

Let's create our first outbound relay, for unencrypted HTTP traffic. Start with a relay listening on the local host.

```
relay "proxy" {
  listen on 127.0.0.1 port 8080
  forward to destination
}
```

You could put this on an IP that faces the network, but there's no reason to. This kind of application is exactly what localhost was invented for.

The key part here is the `forward to destination` line. A diversion leaves the original packet unchanged. The relay can grab the original IP packets and use them to look up where this traffic should go.

Now you need to steer traffic to this proxy. Add a final rule to your *pf.conf*.

```
pass in on inside inet proto tcp to port 80 \
  divert-to 127.0.0.1 port 8080
```

This permits TCP port 80 traffic to enter the host. The divert-to parameter tells PF to steer any traffic to port 80 to port 8080 on the local host. Reload both PF and relayd and test with a browser. Congratulations, you have an outbound relay proxy!

This simple proxy looks indistinguishable from a NAT device, however. If the client is using a packet sniffer, it'll even show that the traffic is going to its original destination. To prove it's a proxy, add a filter.

```
http protocol "dangitbill" {
  return error
  block request url "www.mallard.info/" \
    label "Get to work!"
}
```

If the relay is successfully creating new TCP connections and examining requests at the application layer, a user attempting to reach this site will get a browser error. You want to block Facebook and Twitter? That's pretty straightforward now. Except for the part where both sites use TLS and not unencrypted HTTP, requiring a different approach…

TLS Interception

The whole point of TLS is that it provides confidentiality and data integrity during transport. You can't just stick a piece of middleware in the connection and inspect what's in the data stream.

Unless the desktop client already trusts a TLS certificate for your organization, that is. Then you can have your relay request TLS-protected pages for the client, decrypt them, apply any filters, and re-sign the original page with the organization's certificate. This works exactly like any other proxy, with the added bonus of dynamic re-signing of content.

Your relayd host needs a copy of the organization's private certificate, the private key, and the password (if any). If you work at an actual Certificate Authority, just install the official certificate and private key on your relayd box. That'll greatly simplify client deployment. If you don't have a private CA certificate and key, you'll need to make one.

You also need coherent time across your network. Clients reject certificates signed in the future. Fixing your organization's clocks is beyond the scope of this book.

As I write this, though, interception isn't transparent for TLS sites that use SNI. SNI support should be available in OpenBSD 6.2. Adding SNI might cause minor configuration changes, but they'll be documented in the man pages and any example files.

Your Private CA

Clients trust files and transactions signed by a trusted key. By creating a CA for your organization and installing the CA certificate on your clients, you can tell clients to trust anything you sign.

Many organizations already have a private certificate authority. If you're in a large organization, check and see if a private CA already exists before creating a new one. The organization CA certificate will already be installed on the client systems. While the security team shouldn't trust any random sysadmin with the organization's key, they will probably be willing to give you an intermediate key that can sign other certs.

If you search the Internet you can probably find globally recognized certificates, with private keys and passphrases, that clever people extracted from badly designed embedded systems. Using such a key in your relay would eliminate the need to distribute the private certificate. These keys might get revoked at any time, however, and their use is legally questionable. I would encourage you to expend the effort to distribute your private CA. Forget the legalities, relying on a leaked key that might get revoked during the middle of a big company event causes meetings.

If no private CA exists, create one yourself with openssl(1).

```
# openssl req -x509 -days 365 -newkey rsa:2048 \
  -keyout /etc/ssl/private/ca.key -out /etc/ssl/ca.crt
```

As OpenSSL command lines go, this one isn't actively nightmarish. You're requesting a new X.509 certificate, valid for 365 days. (You might find extending the lifetime convenient, but don't lazily add a zero to make it a whole ten years. Go for two or three years, even though it means doing actual multiplication.) You're asking for a new 2048-bit RSA key. The key goes in /etc/ssl/private/ca.key, while the certificate goes in /etc/ssl/ca.crt. It requests a passphrase. I gave this one *komodia*,[31] and then it goes through the usual TLS certificate questions.

```
Country Name (2 letter code) []: US
State or Province Name (full name) []: Michigan
Locality Name (eg, city) []: Detroit
Organization Name (eg, company) []: Mark Allard Memorial Int'l
Organizational Unit Name (eg, section) []:
Common Name (eg, fully qualified host name) []: mallard.info
Email Address []: webmaster@mallard.info
```

You'll now have a private certificate authority. I'd explain how to sign other certificates with it, except that relayd does all that for you.

Distribute the file /etc/ssl/ca.crt to all of your clients.

---

31   A purely random word that really and truly has no association *whatsoever* with any leaked CA-level certificates.

Relay Certificate

The relay will listen with TLS, so it needs a certificate. The actual certificate the client will receive comes from the destination site: relayd only needs enough of a certificate to perform some basic setup before forwarding the server's re-signed certificate. Don't even bother with ACME; use a self-signed certificate here. Here I create a self-signed certificate for port 8443 on `localhost`.

```
# openssl req -nodes -x509 -days 3652 -newkey \
  rsa:2048 -keyout /etc/ssl/private/127.0.0.1:8443.key \
  -out /etc/ssl127.0.0.1:8443.crt
```

Yes, I'm lazy. This key is good for ten years, including two leap years. But it never actually gets used, so that's okay.

Configuring Relayd for Interception

We already have a relay and protocol for intercepting port 80. Intercepting port 443 is very similar.

```
http protocol "intercept" {
  return error
  tls ca cert "/etc/ssl/ca.crt"
  tls ca key "/etc/ssl/private/ca.key" \
    password "komodia"
  pass url log
}

relay "tlsintercept" {
  listen on 127.0.0.1 port 8443 tls
  protocol intercept
  forward with tls to destination
}
```

The protocol "intercept" gives the path to the certificate, the key, and the password to the key.

The relay itself listens on port 8443, with TLS enabled. It calls the protocol "intercept," and forwards the connection onward.

Use a PF rule to intercept traffic.

```
pass in on inside inet proto tcp to port 443 \
    divert-to 127.0.0.1 port 8443
```

Reload both PF and relayd, and you'll start intercepting traffic.

What the Client Sees

When the client requests an SSL-protected page, such as https://mallard.info, relayd intercepts the request. It makes its own request to the destination and filters the response. At that point, relayd re-signs the response with its private CA and hands the response to the client.

The client sees the response signed by a valid certificate. The browser still sees the friendly padlock we've taught our users to expect from "secure" web sites. The change is only visible if they view the certificate details, where they'd learn that your private CA signed the certificate.

Relayd as a Proxy

Relayd is an excellent solution for certain classes of problems. It's a general-purpose tool, though, with a limited feature set. As your organization grows, you might find yourself needing more protocol-specific tools. If you eventually need to use a proxy with more protocol-specific features to handle certain traffic, while relying on relayd as a general TCP/IP proxy, that's fine.

Don't let relayd's flexibility bind you. Use the right tool for the job.

Now let's see what relayd can do for high availability and high performance.

Chapter 16: High Availability and High Performance

Distributing load between application servers is a great idea. Using relayd can let you put dozens of hosts into serving a single web site. If one of the web servers breaks, relayd transparently pulls it from the mix. Everything works beautifully until the relayd host breaks and everything fails together. Relayd provides high availability through existing OpenBSD features.

And sometimes, even relayd isn't enough. You've bought the best forty-gigabit network interfaces on the market and stolen a next-generation switch from a manufacturer's research lab, and even then the hardware just can't keep up. OpenBSD lets you cut some corners with Direct Server Return to cope with such ridiculous loads.

Start with high availability.

High Availability and Relayd

OpenBSD's CARP protocols and tools such as pfsync(8) give the operating system a base level of failover ability. OpenBSD provides extensive documentation on their failover features and building a PF-based firewall cluster, but you'll need to consider additional factors when using relayd atop such a cluster.

Relayd supports two different styles of load balancing: redirections and relays. Redirections add rules to PF; relays do not. If you're using redirections, you'll need to make sure that the PF state tables on each cluster host are kept in sync. With relays, all TCP/IP connections terminate on the relay host. OpenBSD can't fail over live TCP/IP sessions.

You can't avoid a certain amount of session breakage when a relay host dies, but you can minimize the time to recovery.

My experience is that our best plans fail once exposed to indifferent reality. You might plan for your relayd box to only use relays, and thus you won't have any need for redirections. Or maybe you expect redirections to handle everything. My guess is that these expectations will last three, maybe four days after you go into production. I strongly encourage you to set up your relayd cluster so that it can handle either sort of failover.

So let's briefly talk about building a PF cluster.

Build a PF Cluster

Chapter 9 introduces CARP. Review that chapter for the essentials. A CARP packet filter is much like a pair of servers using CARP for redundancy, except that the packet filters forward packets and must synchronize TCP/IP state information between them.

Here I present a quick guide to clustering OpenBSD PF packet filters, combined with my own recommendations. If you have any difficulty, I encourage you to look at the PF FAQ or Hansteen's *Book of PF*, which both cover this topic in exhaustive detail.

Wire your hosts into the network in the same way: if host **relay1** has interface ix0 facing the Internet and ix1 facing your server farm, plug in the interfaces on **relay2** so that ix0 and ix1 are facing the same networks. A few seconds of changing wiring now will prevent Future You from cursing the day of your birth. Each host needs one network interface or VLAN for each network that it's attached to. Ideally, you'll have another dedicated to communication between the hosts.

Once the hosts are physically identical, install them identically, exactly as you would for CARP between servers.

Each host needs identical packet filter rules. The PF rules discussed in Chapter 9 are a decent place to start. CARP is TCP/IP protocol number 112—no, not port 112, protocol 112, just like TCP is protocol 6 and UDP is protocol 17. You'll need a PF rule to pass CARP and pfsync traffic on each interface. You'll also need a rule to pass pfsync(5) traffic on whatever interface you're using to synchronize traffic.

```
pass quick proto carp
pass quick on em1 proto pfsync
```

Time spent configuring your hosts properly before they go live will save you boundless trouble later. You think you're tired now? Wait until you have to fix an unexpected outage at 3 AM, you'll tell you what tired is!

CARP normally relies on the host's state to determine if it should claim the master role or not. A host might be up and running without relayd running on the host. In this case, you don't want the host to claim the CARP master role. Relayd uses CARP demotion to pass availability information to the host. CARP demotion lets a host throw up its hands and say "Nope, I'm not ready to be the master." This requires preemption. Set the sysctl `net.inet.carp.preempt` to 1 in `/etc/sysctl.conf` on both hosts.

```
net.inet.carp.preempt=1
```

You'll also need a pfsync(5) interface to synchronize the state table between your relayd hosts. Here's an `/etc/hostname.pfsync0` that attaches the virtual pfsync interface to my inside interface, em1, and exchanges updates with the other host in the cluster at 192.0.2.12.

```
syncdev em1 syncpeer 192.0.2.12 up
```

You'll need an identical `relayd.conf` on both hosts, including load balancer options. Algorithms that use hashes need the same hash on both hosts.

That's all pretty standard. Let's see how relayd hooks into all this.

Relayd and PF Demotion

Relayd can increment the demotion counter when all the hosts in a table become unreachable. Use the *demote* option and the name of the interface group in the relay configuration. Remember, all CARP interfaces default to being in the interface group carp.

```
redirect www {
    listen on 203.0.113.211 tcp port 80
    forward to <www> check http "/" code 200 demote carp
}
```

Other processes besides relayd can demote and undemote CARP groups, however. You'll need to check for clashes between processes to make sure they're not squabbling over which host gets to be in charge.

Direct Server Return

Sometimes the best hardware you can get isn't sufficient to the load. On other sites, the best hardware that *exists* can't hack it. That's where Direct Server Return, or DSR, comes in.

A normal redirection passes all traffic through the relayd host. A request comes in from a client. Relayd steers the request to an application server. The response returns to the relayd box, and then to the client.

DSR cuts the relayd box out of the return trip. The incoming request arrives at the relayd box and is sent to the application server as usual, but then the application server replies directly to the client. The trick here is that each application server has two network interfaces, each attached to the same network as the relayd box. Suppose the relayd machine has a public IP of 203.0.113.2 and a private IP of 192.0.2.2. The first application server might have a public IP of 203.0.113.101 and a private IP of 192.0.2.101, the second 203.0.113.102 and 192.0.2.102, and so on. All of the systems, relayd host and application servers alike, use a default gateway on the 203.0.113.0/24 network.

This lets the application servers forge replies from the relayd host's public IP.

Direct Server Return works only with redirects. You can't use DSR with relays.

DSR weakens network-layer security. PF only sees half of each TCP/IP session, so it can provide only minimal protection to the application servers. PF calls this *sloppy state*. Sloppy state isn't nearly as careful as PF's normal stateful inspection, but on the other hand, it's roughly comparable to the stateful inspection found in some other implementations. I'm not saying sloppy state isn't bad, merely that it's only about as bad as some others' best efforts.

Any daemons listening on the application servers' public-facing addresses are exposed to the Internet. I strongly recommend carefully configuring PF on each server's public interface to deny all connections from the outside world.

You are almost always better served by buying bigger hardware. If you can't increase your hardware, though, here's how you set up DSR. You'll need to make changes on both the relayd host and the application servers.

DSR Redirects

Configuring a DSR relay uses the *route to* option. Where forward to rewrites each incoming packet in traditional NAT style, this option routes each packet to an application server using PF's route-to feature. You must also specify the interface you want the packets to leave the relayd host on. Here, interface vmx1 hooks the host to the private network, and the public IP is 203.0.113.211.

```
redirect www {
    listen on 203.0.113.211 tcp port 80
    route to <www> check http "/" code 200 interface vmx1
}
```

Connections coming in for 203.0.113.211 are routed to the application servers in the table www, as the load balancing algorithm dictates. Now to get those hosts to accept those packets.

DSR Application Servers

Hosts know their own IP addresses. When a packet arrives with a destination IP other than theirs, they ignore it. It's not their business. The trick with DSR it to give the load balancer's public-facing IP address to every application server in the farm. You can't attach that IP to an interface on the network, though—we've all seen those "MAC address such-and-such is using my IP, the filthy monster!" warnings.

The trick is to attach the relayd host's public IP to the loopback interface. Addresses on that interface don't go into the ARP table. When a packet for that IP arrives, the host accepts it as its own. OpenBSD doesn't have an */etc/hostname.lo0* file, though, so you can't readily configure the loopback interface on its own. The simplest way to make the change is to attach the lo0 configuration to another network interface. Remember, you can enter arbitrary shell commands in an */etc/hostname* file by putting an exclamation point in front of the command.

Here I configure a web server's */etc/hostname.vmx0* interface with a public IP, and I add an alias for the relayd host's to lo0.

```
inet 203.0.113.201/24
!ifconfig lo0 alias 203.0.113.213/32
```

Be sure the host's default route points at the external router, and your DSR is ready to fly!

Afterword

All web servers are terrible. Load balancers are worse. The nature of networking and application protocols basically demand that any tool that supports either will be ghastly.

Httpd and relayd are merely less terrible.

Neither tool is a perfect fit for all situations. Sometimes you'll require features only found in more complicated software. But httpd and relayd are sufficient for the vast majority of web sites.

After years in systems administration, even my bones have realized that having all the features is… not a feature. Features mean flaws. Every feature can interact with every other feature, exponentially increasingly the software's complexity. Every increase of complexity increases the odds of a critical service randomly going belly-up at a really inconvenient time. (I'm also fairly certain that "really inconvenient time" detection is a feature secretly added to software. But maybe that's just my paranoia talking.)

Conversely, a lack of features *is* a feature. Enjoy your peace and quiet.

Never miss a new Lucas release!

Sign up for Michael W Lucas' mailing list.
https://mwl.io

More Tech Books from Michael W Lucas

Absolute BSD
Absolute OpenBSD (1st and 2nd edition)
Cisco Routers for the Desperate (1st and 2nd edition)
PGP and GPG
Absolute FreeBSD
Network Flow Analysis
Absolute FreeBSD 3rd edition (coming 2018)

the IT Mastery Series

SSH Mastery (1st and 2nd edition)
DNSSEC Mastery
Sudo Mastery
FreeBSD Mastery: Storage Essentials
Networking for Systems Administrators
Tarsnap Mastery
FreeBSD Mastery: ZFS
FreeBSD Mastery: Specialty Filesystems
FreeBSD Mastery: Advanced ZFS
PAM Mastery
Relayd and Httpd Mastery
Ed Mastery

Novels (as Michael Warren Lucas)

git commit murder
Immortal Clay
Kipuka Blues
Butterfly Stomp Waltz
Hydrogen Sleets

Sponsors

The following great people thought this book was important enough that they offered me financial support as I wrote it. Ebook sponsors paid at least $20 for the privilege of getting their name in the electronic version, while the folks who sponsored the print version coughed up at least $100 to have their name immortalized in dead trees.

I appreciate you all. Thank you very much.

Carlin Bingham
Alex Bartlett
Mischa Peters
Stefan Johnson
Andrew Dekker
Phi Network Systems
Adam McDougall
Wolfram Regen
RD Thrush
Zann Ali
Mason Egger
Jim Thompson
Anthony Carpenter

Made in the USA
Las Vegas, NV
30 November 2022